TRAPPED BY HISTORY

the remaking of America and death of the middle class

H.T. Scott Gibbons

H.T. Scott Gibbons

Contents

Preface

In earlier years I had expected to write using extensive references and comparison according to current standard methods and approach, but at the present stage of world development I think the best and most effective way to explore the nature of the modern world is through a more relaxed tract style of writing that does not place too many demands on documentation and format. Such a relaxed style of writing was the most common for broad understanding until the most recent times, and delivers the historically most influential writings that until recently formed the core of our civilization. A relaxed literary style allows for free thinking and rational exploration methods that are restricted by the pseudo-scientific writing style that prevails today. More importantly, by discarding the research and citation method of writing, it allows a focus on the writer's actual observations and experiences, rather than on the possibly incorrect or unverified writings (often well documented by biased or ideological references) of others.

This book does not claim to conform to any discipline such as history, political science or sociology. Accordingly, the influence of, but not comparison with, thinkers unconstrained by rigid discipline such as Michel Foucault, Raymond Aron and Daniel Bell, may be felt. Ultimately, the purpose of this book is to perform a long overdue spring cleaning of accepted ideas and explanations underlying American society, and to carry on the search for honesty, truth and meaning in everyday life.

The reader of this book is given a single guide to this and all analysis: only that which has been seen, credibly validated and can be reasonably supported by the individual himself or by a traditional proper chain of truly trustworthy and capable individuals should be accepted in itself and for use in evaluating other observations. Long live truth and may illusion be unveiled.

H.T. Scott Gibbons

Chapter 1. The Historical Struggle of the Middle Class

Power elite rule was the dominant political structure until its apparent decline beginning with the American Revolution in the late 18th century. By the end of World War II, it *appeared* to have all but vanished but for minor symbolic representations in some European countries and tribal societies. This has generally been presented and understood to be the result of the advent of the so-called democratic age in which power elite rule was replaced by rule with the consent and participation of the governed. Apparently by coincidence, the democratic age occurred at the same time as the world entered into the modern era of unprecedented urbanization, population sizes and population growth. As a result the world was trapped by history.

The distinctive religious, landed, ethnic and military forms of power elite rule can be conceptually and historically lumped together since they are the only structural type of rule (as opposed to governance) that had been experienced in most of history, except perhaps in ancient Greece and some primitive societies. With this statement I make a distinction between a necessary hierarchical social organization with democratic elites (based on the middle classes), and a non-democratic power elite rule. In particular I suggest that the ideological basis for the United States was the concept of a widely participatory society organized and managed by a regularly affirmed/changed membership of a moderately hierarchical social/ruling structure with no fixed membership. This is what made the United States system historically different.

The real distinction of the American political economy was that while rule was still by an elite, it was not an extreme (socially and economically isolated), international, independent or fixed power elite, but *a national network of local elites with allegiance to and dependence on a largely self-directed and self-reliant middle class population of shared experience and culture, which had control of its own sufficient resources and relative freedom of action.* These population characteristics cannot be overemphasized and were historically unique, in considerable part due to the large area of North American settlement and nearly unlimited resources.

Even from the earliest colonial times the American people were not fully under the control of the British monarch, and had the ability and resources to resist efforts made against its interests. The people who guided the American Revolution ultimately made a local interest-based *nationalistic* choice to divorce from Britain, but this was not necessarily a choice to renounce the colonial *form* of hierarchical society, but rather to install civil leadership through an advanced middle class form of the Cromwellian parliament as local ruling classes in a *national hierarchy*. In fact, there was at least some support for and effort even to install a national power elite rule along aristocratic lines similar to those in England. According to the American myth, those efforts failed and a mild and moderately hierarchical rule was established and sanctioned by the middle classes (aka "the people") through what has come to be understood as the American democratic process.

Democratic hierarchical rule was largely supported by a broad-based core of literate, land-owning, tax-paying, white free men, who filled the increasing and expanding ruling positions. There were some outside of this core group that did not support hierarchical rule and the expanded role of government that supported it. This was most notably demonstrated in the Whiskey Rebellion by common people against central regulation and taxation of private action and enterprise by the government, during the tenure of President George Washington, almost immediately after American Independence.

If the suppression of the Whiskey Rebellion by the Federal Government did not demonstrate that the practice and structure (as opposed to the form and personalities) of power elite or statist rule had not really changed, the Indian Removal (mainly of the advanced Cherokee Nation) and the War of Northern Aggression clearly should have. In the case of the War of Northern Aggression, not only was the will of the voting majority in nearly half of the American states rejected, but those states were compelled to surrender the rights of local independence that all the colonies had jointly fought for less than a century before.

How could such a shocking reversal come to be? Rather than accepting the *stated objectives* for such government actions (such as ensuring adherence to law, protecting the lives of settlers and eliminating slavery), the authentic motivation behind such harsh actions should be understood from the *results,* which were the empowerment of the modern industrial and financial (and empire-building) power elite at the expense of the broad middle class, and the traditional independent and agrarian sectors. As a result of these actions *some benefits* from the stated objectives were obtained by *some groups*, but the more important benefits came less visibly from the unstated objectives, and for the *power elite (or initially, powerful interests)* for which the *openly benefitting groups* were only pawns and coincidental tools. The fundamental *unstated objective* was to control resources (rule) by a small power elite which was not necessarily incompatible with governing through a middle class-controlled hierarchical structure, because it could be achieved without total control of government and society.

This unstated objective was often achieved through the dispossession and disenfranchisement of groups that controlled resources obstructing or desired by some of the hierarchical rulers (who gradually became the American power elite as centralized government interests merged with those of big finance and industry) continued into the 20th Century most notably with Native Americans, but ultimately with Southerners, whites, males, English Speakers and other groups controlling resources and influence that could challenge power elite rule as had been done in the struggle for American Independence. Specific challenges to the power elite were made periodically by labor, Native Americans, survivalists, Southern Segregationists, anti-busing families, the Civil Rights Movement and anti-war activists, but these challenges appear to have largely ended in the 1970s. Numerous indirect propagandistic challenges against *social norms* (not the same as opposition to the *power elite*) as well as the audacious direct challenges made by the youth movement, homosexuals and illegal aliens (discussed in later chapters) cannot be placed in the same category as opposition to elite power, since these challenges were largely elite-supported or elite-supporting challenges to the middle class social consensus (not all rebellion against established customs, laws and social preferences is anti-elite and may paradoxically be pro-elite under current conditions).

For almost 200 years the American democratic elite (as distinct from the power elite) endured, expanded, matured and broadened, but largely remained dependent on the middle class, and on the continually expanded and broadened voting population and its cultural base, as well as its relatively short period of dependence on labor. Of course there was certainly a transition from a literate European, Protestant, white male base to a less literate European, Protestant-Catholic white male and female base which retained a diminished but still extensive core identity. It was the growing power of the labor movement and the so-called Civil Rights Movement (CRM) that began to drive a wedge within the traditional body politic, which greatly expanded with the youth, women's, sexual, and diversity movements, and with immigration from countries outside of Northern and Western Europe.

Democratic elite dependence on local constituencies with shared values continued to some extent until sometime perhaps in the 1980s or about the time of the election of Bill Clinton as President (Incidentally, Clinton was from Arkansas and George Bush from Texas, being the last two presidents to conform to the dubious recent popular wisdom that a only a president from a Sunbelt state could be elected. The election of Barrack Obama, in particular, has shown that the theory of Sunbelt power could not be fully validated). This dependence on local constituencies with shared values had marked the American democratic elite as different from power elites elsewhere in the world, and shaped the flawed concepts and expectations of American politics held by people around the world.

However, as noted by New York Times columnist David Brooks in Bobos in Paradise, and in Paradise Road, the American democratic elite underwent a fundamental and massive change between 1950 and 2000 whereby it delinked from its historical dependence on region, culture and ethnicity – and labor, becoming either part of the power elite, or agents of the power elite, rather than "the people." I suggest that the reason it could do this was primarily the post-World War II establishment of the United States Dollar as the world's reserve currency and the deregulation/financial manipulation, historically unique in scale and event, that freed power elite assets (and behavior) from physical, spatial and cultural restrictions and largely changed the trajectory of American society toward a society where there was *no middle class force capable of mounting a challenge to the power elite*.

Stepping back in time we should ask what happened to the old, eclipsed, mainly European, aristocracy? Of course many of them failed to board the train for the modern era (of expanded population, education, health and affluence) and wasted their assets to the extent that they became irrelevant. Others, however, made the transition through education, investment and political activity.

Many of the old elite had international and interlinking marriage alliances in addition to national power. This allowed the European balance of power system to endure into the 20th Century.

Some, but not all of the pre-democracy elite wealth of Europe did disappear with the change to so-called democratic systems or even with the two world wars. To the contrary, Europe's elites rebounded to challenge those of the United States within a little over 20 years of the end of World War II and its massive destruction. This process of elite restoration is presented by Thomas Piketty in Capital in the Twenty-First Century. Beyond Piketty's analysis, is there also some characteristic of European national wealth hidden outside mere physical measure? To further explore the reasons for successful cultures the reader may wish to read Jared Diamond's Collapse. It is noteworthy that old European (and American) elites are less visible today than are new elites, but they may still be sharing power discretely. It may also be that international elites are now more active in the new global economy than in their home countries.

The nature of the new or greatly mutated American democratic elite of the post-World War II era began to show similarities with the old European elite that had been thought extinct. Interlinking alliance marriages without reference to region, nation, religion or even culture have become the rule among the American democratic elite within two generations (as noted in Bobos in Paradise by David Brooks and in Coming Apart: the State of White America 1960-2010 by Charles Murray), setting the American democratic elite free from traditional American social control.

The only requirement for the new elite now is *just to be a member of the elite*, meaning educated, famous, rich or powerful, and it no longer carries a cultural, regional or biological connection. I first learned how this works when a graduate of Harvard College and Law and my Berkeley graduate studies co-fellow regaled me with stories of the children of the famous or unique - but not of the educated or traditional elite - who were admitted to elite schools. This creation of a new heterogeneous, non-democratic elite, delinked from any other groups is one of the key objectives of the so-called affirmative action programs as well as the Rhodes Scholarship and other such programs.

The American democratic elite has always been larger than the old European elite and was based more on education, profession and financial (not necessarily land) wealth, which had to be constantly recreated each generation, but this need for re-creation has been rapidly reduced since World War II. The new American elite is the model for new elites around the world which are increasingly linked together from nation to nation. Increasingly elites of two nationalities or allegiances are married and enjoy the benefits of power in one or more countries of their choosing (this was presaged in the 1980 book The Third Wave by Alvin Toffler). Elite alienation from place has made that class largely immune from local and community control under the pretext of meritocracy and independent professionalism. As a result, the new elite rule has taken on the structural form of historical elite rule rather than of the American democratic elite.

The middle class has increasingly faced regulation and other financial, certification and behavioral control by this new elite, which has narrowed its freedom, independence and ultimate political power. The most glaring examples of this elite power are the increased and increasingly restrictive government regulations such as zoning, controls, standards, and education/job certification.

The increasing use of credit (not simple borrowing, but the capitalization and dedication of streams of income for individual lifetimes) and urbanization have exacerbated the impact of elite control through regulation and ultimately have enslaved most of the working population as perpetual dual wage earners and resume builders with little job security or freedom to exit from the system. Power elites and their agents have been further refining their control over umbrella financial instruments and procedures, and also the actual valuation of assets and labor through currency control and manipulation. The nexus of the Federal Reserve, the United States Treasury Department and other government agencies can decide - outside of public accountability and an independent market mechanism - how to calculate inflation, what interest rates to set and how to value companies and financial instruments. In so doing, they actually set the absolute value of all private assets and labor.

A quick example of this is the government policy of setting interest rates, Although not well appreciated, this in effect sets the value of savings assets even including housing and cash. The annual interest earned on $100,000 at the current 1 per cent rate would be $1,000 compared with $10,000 at a more reasonable inflation compensating 10 per cent rate. What this really means is that not just current earning is reduced ($9,000 less), but that if an individual is not a spender of wages, but rather an investor of assets to use as income, it would take $1,000,000 to earn the same amount that would have been earned by $100,000 only a few years ago, keeping most other cost/value factors the same. As a result, it is not just the $9,000 interest return each year that is lost, but a conceptual loss of the additional $900,000 that would be required to produce that current earning without capital depletion. In such a scenario, the elites who can benefit from low interest rates, for whatever reasons (such as the government being able to borrow at a lower cost, and stock market speculators), will receive this huge transfer of wealth from the middle class.

This is not a hypothetical case, but a reflection of the actual situation. It is shocking, but shows how elites can use government policy to erase almost any amount of private asset value by altering the underlying financial rules and policy. It is not merely elite and

16

government control of the day to day visible economic system functions such as operating law and regulations, but even the most fundamental definition and functions of the financial system that are now altered to benefit or harm the middle class.

There is an often overlooked distinction between the power elites with extreme wealth and power that benefit greatly from political and economic control, and the neo-elite managers that merely implement that control and escape the greatest disabilities of power elite rule as long as they can provide support services. It is often argued that so many neo-elites could not possibly be involved in implementation of a diabolical broad-based program to oppress and disenfranchise the middle class, since such people would necessarily include our nice ordinary friends and neighbors - people just like us.

However, involvement by that large technical-management class is possible because those neo-elites are not merely benefiting from the opportunities of the steadily ratcheted up control system, but also because they have some amnesty from total disempowerment by virtue of being the system's implementing agents, and not having any fixed interests which can be compromised. In such a system many or all of the power elite do not have to micro-conceive or manage all aspects of the oppressive system since it is self-perpetuating through the interests of the technical-management class. As such the system is not a power elite conspiracy, but a management structure.

In such an environment who would the power elites actually be? They would not necessarily be a genetic cabal as in the past (although Charles Murray argues in Coming Apart that they are well on their way to being this), but those who can greatly benefit from the centralization, specialization, technologization and control of the great majority of modern people. They would be those who secondarily seek to remove all obstacles and resistance to their control from any groups or ideologies. Anything that breaks up social cohesion and local control will favor power elite rule, even if substantial short term (or even long term) benefits to certain other non-elite groups can and do result.

Practical application of such divide and rule approaches can be seen in the fragmented and confusing maze of the post-British colonial world, but those appear clumsy and impermanent in comparison with similar techniques in the advanced economic sectors. It is in those advanced economic sectors where traditional identities are already weak, and social organization is mainly through transitory associations which lack the strength to create and maintain identity and allegiance. The middle class of earlier times was created under different conditions and functioned effectively for many generations, largely through family, tribe, guild and community. However, those social unities have irrevocably broken down. Now that most of the world economy has been brought under global elite control, developing or restoring span of control for identities and allegiances would be a huge and daunting task.

It can be seen why and how power elites have taken control of American society with increasing rapidity and extent. This book will review and consider the process and methods used to achieve control over the American political economy (but which have not been seen for their true nature as they unfolded) and assess the current the current state of the middle class social contract in America.

Chapter 2. A Re-assessment of American History Based on Outcomes Not Ideology

From Colonial Days to the War of Northern Aggression

Throughout history freedom for most ordinary people in most of the world has been constrained regardless of the political, economic or social system, simply by virtue of limited land and resources (and with the associated greed). This situation really began to change with the European discovery of vast lands which were sparsely settled and at a lower level of technical development. Frontier countries such as Canada, the United States, Australia, South Africa, New Zealand, Brazil, Argentina, etc. provided land and resources that could be possessed afresh, thus creating "new" wealth that could not be replicated in well-established countries. So, while possession of land and resources in established states depended on inheritance, social control, power - and only in recent times, cleverness and financial manipulation - possession of land in the frontier countries was mainly achieved simply by being quick to act, early to arrive, and by manipulation of legal (land registry), technical (ground survey), and social (slavery, indenture) tools.

As a result, much wealth in the frontier states was "new wealth" rather than reallocated "old wealth." Since the terms of wealth acquisition were different in the frontier states than in the established states, it is not so useful to compare the quality of their government and economic systems and participants independently of other factors such as social control, ease of mobility and uncontrolled resources, although this is in fact what has generally been done.

Since frontier states had larger geographic spaces that were newly acquired and more difficult to control than earlier densely settled areas in Europe, the inhabitants had more freedom, although this was always tempered by the desire of new elites to exert control. During the frontier colonization period the world system was really in a state of flux and modernizing. Although some established states began to allow more freedom for some of their citizens, the most notable beneficiaries of this period were the people in frontier societies or regions rather than those in old established states.

This book focuses on how this situation affected the history and development of the United States and brought us to our current situation. The stages of development in America can be summarized as exploration, resource harvesting, farming, labor production, urbanization, industrialization, technical development, and finally today; rentier economy.

The American Founding Fathers were by no means saints and often were greedy, self-serving actors, caring little for the interests of others and competing fiercely for any unclaimed resources even to the extent of manipulating laws, rules and procedures in their favor. Much land in the United States was claimed by founding fathers and various nation builders, and snatched by them from ordinary people until recent years when most frontier land ceased to be of interest to the power elite. In recent years the less crude tool of regulation has been used to gain control of and profits from the land for the power elite.

In America the social and political foundation of the early years was an amalgam of the early settlers, cultures and philosophies current in the tumultuous mid-18th Century. What was notable about this foundation was that it provided a structure and framework for organizing a diverse society with a common purpose of working for personal improvement and independence. This common purpose was shared in diverse constituencies such as (don't tread on me) self-reliant poor whites, soldiers of fortune, lesser nobility and utopians, but was loosely managed by the colonial elite that transcended all others by virtue of its erudition and financial capacity.

The original settlers of the American Colonies came from various backgrounds with various objectives, both good and bad. There were fortune seekers, religious zealots, surplus population, social misfits, etc. Overall, this group wanted new opportunities and to be free from coercion and control. That did not mean they were necessarily averse to dominating others, or that they were saints, only that they generally looked forward to opportunities rather than backward to past wrongs and mistakes.

One of the most important observations made about the colonial population at the time of Independence is that most white, adult males were literate. While many of the most clever and sociable colonists settled in towns and near the Atlantic Coast, even in the early days there were those who sought free (unclaimed) spaces for living, no matter how distant or difficult. Those less socialized people joined Native Americans, and various bands of Spanish and other non-North Americans including Africans in making lives on the frontier.

America was anything but stable in the colonial period, and coastal population growth brought about increased government organization and geographic expansion. The frontier constantly expanded, ultimately pushing many misfits further from the coast and from the benefits of urban society. Many of the founding fathers were keen investors and capital accumulators. Because of their education and residence in or near government centers, the founding fathers were often involved in allocation, management and claiming of land in expanded frontier jurisdictions as elected representatives, land surveyors or speculators. For them this work involved mainly field surveys or administrative work on paper rather than occupation or development of land, but the impact was to continually dispossess those who had no knowledge of government procedures or effective access to them. The dispossessed were most famously the Cherokee Indians, mixed races, and the Scots-Irish.

Conflicting interests in mercantile sea trade policy were probably the major reason for the War for American Independence rather than explanations from high flown ideology and myth. *It is not by the identity of its supporters that one must judge a movement, but by the authentic cause of its origin and theoretical development (almost any ideology can be supported by any group at any time given suitable conditions, and with no internal conflict).* Most pre-revolutionary seaborne trading by Colonial Americans was done in the Caribbean and other regional areas of the Americas as a small scale activity that individual entrepreneurs could engage in. Britain largely controlled the higher investment trans-Atlantic sea trade. By the time of the War for American Independence elites in American wanted to protect their regional trade and local profits, as well as to expand into the world trade stage. It is likely that this ambition was the real reason for the revolution rather than taxes or the nature of the British monarchy. After all, why should frontiersmen worry so much about taxes or the King when they made most of their own possessions?

As the War for American Independence neared, there were five main groups in the colonies: Native Americans, Africans, British colonial administrators, settler colonials and frontiersmen. Settler colonials could be divided into large land owners, merchants, craftsmen, yeomen farmers and laborers (including indentured servants). The fundamental challenge in the movement for American independence was for the settler colonial elites to organize the other settler colonials against the British, to counter British alliances with Native Americans, keep African slaves under control, to gain French support and to harass the British through frontiersmen.

The core objective of increased profit and trade for American colonials was not automatically achieved with independence from Britain, or as easy as it often appears in dramatized form. Shortly after victory over the British there were several events such as the

Whiskey Rebellion that showed the conflicting objectives of some of the Independence gang. In short, many of the Independence gang continued to seek the general freedom from government and for the self-sufficiency they had always wanted, while the elites, or wannabe elites, sought to use and expand government for their own interests. The elites covered a wide range of personalities including rapacious self-servers such as Alexander Hamilton, as well as apparently saintly figures such as George Washington. Elites could favor more or less government, but ultimately they were the *party* of government.

It could be said that the limited government group was mainly rural, agricultural and Southern. This group also included frontiersmen, when they intersected with government at all, and the Cherokee (especially the mixed-race people who claimed to be Cherokee through the matrilineal tradition). The populist movement that resulted in the election of Andrew Jackson brought the two post-Independence societies into stark contrast, but ultimately the frontier masses could not find time for politics, and continued their migration westward and to the fringes of society, leaving the formal political struggle to the modernizing Northern capitalists and the Southern agrarians in the period leading up to the War of Northern Aggression.

Agricultural goods production and small time regional trading were quickly consolidated in the Southern states and depended on slave labor, and to a much lesser extent on white yeoman farmers. A generally temperate climate allowed the Southern economy to provide a comparatively satisfactory life for most of its people. Climatic conditions in the Northern states were not so benevolent, yet mainly because of the larger number of suitable ports, immigration there continued to increase and was absorbed by industry, created to some extent by the need to stay warm and inside in the winter.

By the time of the War of Northern Aggression the value of agriculture and mercantile trading had begun to be surpassed by the value of industry in the Northern states and the country as a whole. Partly imported from Europe by new immigrants, and partly stimulated by colonial invention enabled by the free time and resources to experiment with and opportunities to use new techniques and technologies, factory-based industry began to emerge in America, mainly in the Northeast and Mid-Atlantic coastal regions.

As in the conflict between the American Colonies and the British homeland when the American elites developed larger aspirations and the interests of the two began to conflict, a conflict now arose between agrarian Southerners and industrial/trading Northerners because tariff policies could only favor one of those two interests. The conflict was essentially about whose interests the government should promote. Southern interests were less complicated than Northern interests so it appeared they were for limited government in principle. It also appeared that they had some ideological interest in slavery when in fact this was only one factor in their economy just as immigration and lack of worker rights were in the North. Interestingly, it was Northern Abolitionists, rather than White Southerners (the vast majority of whom were small or non slave-owning) that started and financed the "back to Africa" transfer of slaves to West Africa. The War of Northern Aggression was ultimately a national economic structural adjustment rather than an ideological imperative.

After the War of Northern Aggression Until the Great Industrialization

Ultimately (because hardly has any economic structural change ever been completed within any particular historical period), slavery, the agrarian economy and limited government in the South were destroyed by its defeat in the War of Northern Aggression. The

South lost its independent and unique society and began a long journey toward integration with the North and industrialization as a junior partner. Other parts of the country, such as the Midwest, gained stature in the industrial economy, while many areas including the South remained backwaters. These backwaters produced various elected representatives of stature, but most of these were junior partners and focused on regional rather than national interests (rather than the luminaries of the Ante-Bellum and colonial periods).

The relationship of the South with the rest of the country after the War of Northern Aggression was still primarily based on agriculture, but also on some growth in industry from cheap labor, some raw materials, and poorly educated and patriotic army recruits. In order to extract these resources limited national investments were made and the region remained stable if not stagnant.

The cost of the Occupation of the South (so-called Reconstruction) by the power elite-controlled Northern States was ultimately too much of an investment and effort to justify when there were much more valuable areas and activities to be pursued in other parts of the country. If federal laws concerning slavery, and secession could have been postponed until the 1880s, the War might never have happened or the South might have seceded peacefully, because of structural changes in the economy, not because of any change in the ideology of the party of government or social activities. Alas, conflicting interests came to a head just as those interests were about to change.

The Occupation of the South was much less of an effort and expense than the War, and yet, the North tired of it quickly. Abolition had been an ideological movement, based on prosperity, that could be pursued because it did not conflict with the broader economic structure of the United States that came to be dominated by the North. It was easy to be pious about slavery in the North where slavery had no part in the economic and social structure, and where there was no price to be paid, unlike in the South where some Southerners faced a huge financial dilemma in advocating freedom for slaves. As a result, America – one people (mostly) with two economic structures had *evolved* into two ideologies; one a practical one based on economic realities and the other based on self-righteous meddling. This divergence between realism and utopianism would be found from time to time in America on other issues until the present day.

By the end of the War of Northern Aggression, and the Occupation of the South, national resources could be diverted to the challenges and real economic benefits of expanding the United States frontiers to Canada, California and Mexico, and to clearing transportation routes for the emerging massive continental raw materials and factory production economy. This huge effort over such a vast area could not be done wholly by force of arms or machinery. Accordingly the United States Government provided incentives and support such as land grants for the mass colonization, settlement and management of the newly expanded frontier. Shifting emphasis from the Occupation of the South to exploitation of the vast western regions of the country and dispossession of Native Americans was also not an ideological, but a economic structural imperative.

The Government could not have managed such a feat on its own. Only by unleashing the power of new immigrants, Southern economic refugees from war devastation and landless masses, including former slaves, could the land be settled and secured with labor. As a result of the settlement policies of this period, some of the frontier states maintain special forms of government management until the present day. After securing control over Native American activity, raw materials and development of the West Coast and Mississippi River transportation corridors, the Government had little interest in spending its resources on the vast remaining hinterland areas. This was also an economic structural and not an ideological issue.

In summary, the main issues in the early growth of the United States were: expansion of the trading areas and frontiers, development of a national market, open immigration, access to natural resources and plentiful industrial labor. This can be seen as a constantly expanding Adam Smith pie type envelope. Since the type and size of opportunity was constantly expanding there was no need to tinker with a lot of regulation or distribution of resources, since it was not cost effective for the economic and power elite. There were enough benefits in the expansion to satisfy most of the population and keep them occupied. In his book on the Bush Family, American Dynasty, Kevin Phillips documents the rise of the Bush-Prescott Family whose fortunes were also built on that expanding envelope prior to World War I. However, after the end of the American frontier and World War I, interest of the power elite shifted from the domestic frontier to domestic structural control and foreign trade.

World War I, the Roaring 20s, the Great Depression, the New Deal and World War II

A tumultuous period in world history, this period is so replete with events and details that its overall effect on American society is generally overlooked. Two of the most important results of World War I were the extensive direct damage done to the population and resources of Europe, and the relative loss of status of the heavily damaged European industrial assets vis-à-vis the essentially untouched resources of the United States. Just as the labor movement was growing in influence and raising the cost of industrial production in the United States, Europe was damaged by World War I so that America could surge ahead in the roaring twenties. However, greater national economic integration and money supply/investment manipulation destroyed this American advantage when they resulted in the Wall Street stock market crash of 1929.

The resulting Great Depression created major disruptions to American society that were not overcome, but which burdened the society directly, until at least World War II. The great Depression, the Dust Bowl, and the World War II manpower mobilization and industrial conversion had the combined effect of increased dislocation of the population from rural areas and small towns, and reduced individual self-sufficiency and community identity. This was a period of great challenge for America and could have resulted in great national decline, but for unexpected Post-World War II prosperity.

The Post-World War II Economy

Damage to the European and Asian industrial base was much greater in World War II than in World War I. Again the United States entered the War late in the conflict and suffered no damage to its industrial plant. As a result of this the United States emerged as the pre-eminent world industrial power. Returning soldiers were given jobs in the restructured industrial and consumer economy in addition to post-secondary education under the GI Bill. At the same time most consumer goods had become affordable to Americans. The prosperity experienced during this short period was unlike anything that had been known for ordinary people in any previous period of American history, and much, much better than the experience they had from the Wall Street Crash until the end of World War II. The 1950s and early 1960s were anomalous times not truly or fully justified by economic productivity. Yet, during this hubristic era, Americans began to imagine their prosperity was a permanent natural entitlement rather than as a reward that must be earned daily. By setting our current and permanent expectations on this period we imagined that this was the base on which we should build rather than a plateau which must be vigorously defended. Unfortunately, the comfort and illusion of prosperity of that period encouraged social changes and movements that would ultimately make unrealistic demands based on that unrealistic window of time.

In addition to the advantage of an undamaged industrial plant, and unbeknownst to most Americans, this prosperity was also a result of the new Breton Woods world financial structure that used the United States Dollar as the world's reserve currency. That financial structure essentially devalued all other nations' products and wealth on the international (rather than national) market and provided the *second* great American windfall (the *first* being free, low-cost or squatter possession of New World property).

At first this devaluation of other countries' currencies was used to earn profits from skills, assets, resources and (less so) production in other countries for a small few businesses (like ITT and IBM) and traders (such as Pier 1 Imports). This could be seen in the substitution of original Native American souvenir replicas with lower cost imports beginning in the mid-1960s. Even among manufactured goods, low quality Japanese radios were imported at the same time as high quality ones from Europe. That it was possible to purchase both high and low quality goods at relatively low prices should have been the earliest warning to America that this could only be sustained with the United States Dollar as the world reserve currency and with a rentier structure of foreign investment and domination. However, almost no one outside of the highest finance levels considered these issues until Richard Nixon took the United States off the Gold Standard.

For some years after World War II the low level of development of other countries allowed America to export products even with a highly valued Dollar. But as other countries reconstructed and developed (often with United States investment, technology and education) the next step was to use the advantages of the Breton Woods financial system to shift from exporting American products to other countries, to exporting American production to other countries with lower costs, for consumption there as well as for export back to the United States. Lower production costs overseas were made possible by lower absolute costs, but also by the high value of the Dollar. The introduction of massive imports of low cost products created the illusion of prosperity in the United States and allowed consumption to continue and increase at the same time as domestic production (and wealth creation) declined.

Unfortunately, at the same time the nature of lifestyle and consumption changed, and resulted in shifted spending away from durable goods and capital investments to current consumption and intangibles, creating a vicious cycle of spending, using up products and spending again with no ultimate retention of value. Probably even by the mid to late 1950s most of the pent up war time demand (at the pre-war standard with adjustment for improved technology) for durable goods and housing had been fulfilled. As a result, much of the current and potential profit from domestic production was declining for durable goods, except in defense related industries. Yet, lower costs and the vast expansion of credit through the introduction of credit cards generated a higher volume of consumption of consumer products with less tangible or return value, based on expected future income and wealth. As a result our current problems actually started even at the very time when we thought things were going well!

Under these conditions there were only three main structural ways to sustain the high standard of living of this period: beneficial or domineering exchange rate power from the reserve currency; shift of industrial production to military and space applications; and immigration.

The Arab Oil Embargo and the Rise of Petro Dollars

Sometime after the Arab Oil Embargo in the 1970s a new stage in international finance was reached. The idea was that paying more money for oil imports was okay as long as America was the recipient of the reverse spending. Unfortunately, Petro Dollars went to investment and luxury sectors that had little benefit for the middle class. Economists and talking heads began to promote the bogus idea that cheaper manufacture by other countries of the things we didn't want to make was okay as long as all the nice high end service jobs and technical work were ours. This seemed to work for some time as a result of the reserve currency status of the United States Dollar and the desire of exporting nations to export their wealth, and high tech and service expenditure to the United States. But slowly, even the United States market share of high tech goods began to decline. The specialized and limited employment sectors of investment and military equipment continued to be strong, but it was mainly the services market that sustained the American economy because it is more difficult to send much of this work off-shore, and because unprecedented numbers of immigrants came to supplement American labor in that sector, even as similar numbers of native born Americans lost their jobs in productive industry.

Although it is generally considered to be a Republican concept, this new economy of the Clinton Era was predicated on the concept of American Exceptionalism, even though there was little to validate this myth. Still the government under both Democratic and Republican administrations promoted the free trade and trade liberalization that allowed separation of economic resources from physical, geographical and political constraints, with the expectation that all the undesirable work would be done by people in other countries and that the easy work would be done by Americans - or at least by people living in the United States. The practical result of these policies was that wealth could be converted into forms that evaded community and political control. The use of new financial instruments to extract wealth from local communities for investment elsewhere and for importing low-cost products meant a huge loss of localized physical wealth and wealth production at the same time as the money supply and population were greatly expanding.

The End of the Twentieth Century - Bringing the End Game Strategy Together

Recently I watched the movie <u>Meet Me in St Louis</u>. I was amazed by the wonderful house and lifestyle of the family. The family was troubled that, as a middle class family, if they moved to New York from St Louis they would not be able to have as good a life as in St Louis! Looking at the movie and discounting the dream factory effect, I wonder if any family could have such a middle class life in the United States today. It wasn't many yesterdays ago that Americans were intoxicated with our standard of living. Now there seems to be a sense of gloom about the present and the future, but it doesn't appear that much has really changed structurally from the time when we considered ourselves rich and now when that we see an uncertain future ahead. What happened to change things?

Seen in light of actual realities, fundamental American political and economic policies have largely been determined by external conditions and power elites, even though the myth was that they were decided by the people and their representatives. For a long time the interests of the power elite and the independent middle class were not so much in conflict because America and the world were large, and independent space was available for all. The tiny power elite could not directly challenge the middle class for most of American history because of the middle class size and consensus.

The middle class as an absolute independent majority began to decline as a result of the Great Depression and the New Deal. Since World War II massive immigration has introduced ideas alien to those of the native-born Americans as well as shifting the population structure. With this and the growth of government and politically dependent classes, the independent native-born middle class has now become a minority which is no longer capable of defending or even defining shared values. Even the pretender populist movements and leadership of traditional ideology are themselves now more like minority elites than they are representatives of the middle class. Moreover, there is no longer any valid national ideology that can maintain a social contract. Most of the myths that make up the national ideology are not consistent with American history or able to maintain a national identity. The reason is the decline of the middle class majority social contract.

Chapter 3. The Myths of America: Reality Got in the Way

Americans have come to believe that freedom is sacrosanct, prejudice and racism are wrong, crusading reporters and lawyers are selfless and righteous, unbridled capitalism is the most efficient and just economic policy, they are innately smarter, more good and hard working than other people, shared economic interests make the residents of our country citizens, it is right for other countries (but not the United States) to have predominant or traditional identities and self-determination, America should extend rights to nationals of other countries in the United States that are not granted to Americans in those countries, citizenship is just a formality and not an allegiance, people do not have strong bonds with their family and ethnic brothers beyond simple and transparent market relations, our political system is more honest and transparent than others, etc. Some of these conflicting myths are explored in Samuel Huntington's book, Who Are We: The Challenges to America's National Identity.

Another myth of America is that it was a refuge to castoffs from other countries, rather than the historical truth of the ideology of self-reliance and opportunity within a particular cultural and resource exploitation framework. Yet, allowed to remain because it flattered simple minds or because such a huge part of the population was associated with immigration in the later industrial period, this myth became part of and perhaps the most destructive element of the revised American ideology without anyone even knowing.

Each of these myths would deserve a long and detailed exploration, but here we can sum them all up as an American identity that does not support patriotism, nationalism, or nativism. How is it possible to have an American (or any other) national identity supported by these myths? The answer is that no real national identity exists, rather the American society has developed proxies for identity. One of the oldest and increasingly strong proxies is that of market consumerism, especially aspects which are promoted by fads and the advertising industry.

One recent and strange identity proxy is the new glorification of the military as protectors of the homeland, especially since the end of the Cold War. The real questions about the no-draft, volunteer army which go un-asked are whether the military is under civilian control and is it doing work in the interest of the people? Only after we answer these questions can we move on to the question of whether the American army is a mercenary, or a civilian army representing the American people. Today the military has a truly dangerous social composition, is not representative, spawns lobbyists and would be political candidates, and is well down the road to becoming a global Hessian mercenary troupe (non-citizens are allowed in the military and given preferential immigration status) and danger to the civilian population.

Evolution and Change of the American Myth

The American myth was that Americans were smart, hardworking, loyal, moral, religious, family-oriented and productive, but somewhere along the way we became passive consumers, recreational hedonists, and promoters of social misfits, heresies and perversions. Yet, all along the propaganda machines of the right and left elites continued to push their respective versions of American Exceptionalism so that most Americans of all political stripes believed and continued to believe that American prosperity was political and social, not cultural or structural, and resulted from our political institutions, good nature and hard work. This belief denied the importance of any inherited characteristics and only accepted acquired characteristics as if people really are independent of their genetic and cultural backgrounds. As a result of the propagation of this national myth, most Americans came to believe that all native-born Americans - and even immigrants to America - shared these traits and could be partners in the great American venture. It was all one big party and the public did not pause to consider who actually paid for it.

The American Exceptionalism ideology currently in vogue promotes the concept that something has gone wrong with America because our leadership longer believe we are special, but only one of many people among the nations of the world. In light of this, we have to ask whether the American character was exceptional earlier, or whether it was our actual living conditions and our behavioral response that made us special? I would argue that it was the conditions and behavior that made us special, and *only to a much lesser extent that being somehow special produced those conditions and behavior.*

At this stage in our history, how did we end up with this idea of Exceptionalism, and also the opposing idea, apparently promoted by Barack Obama, that we are not exceptional (whatever that means), that do not fit with our actual history, structures and realities? Both of these concepts ignore the unique American conditions and responses to them in favor of myth-making. As with religious fundamentalism, both of these concepts are responses to current conditions with reference *to the past*, rather than validation and reaffirmation *of the past*.

Here would be a good place to consider the ideas in Daniel Bell's, The Post-Technological Society and The Cultural Contradictions of Capitalism which suggest that ideology can become false or self-contradicting over time. Was the original American ideology correct at one time and lost its validity with the passage of time. Was it corrupted or distorted for some reason? Or, have we even been misled even with respect to the original American ideology itself, its history and acceptance?

This book focuses primarily on the United States and how its ideology and social structures have developed. For this we first need to consider the original American ideology? As nicely presented in the book, <u>Founding Brothers</u> by Joseph Ellis, the Founding Fathers had disagreements among themselves, especially between the federalists and state's rights advocates, which have remained the fundamental conflicts in American society.

It is ironic that many supporters of American Independence did not really object to the structure of government by monarchy (statist), only that they themselves wanted to control the government and society, rather than allowing others (such as the king and his supporters) this privilege. This same phenomenon may be found in the independence movements in most former colonies, even though they cloak their political movements in the garb of some noble ideology such as nationalism. Nevertheless, over the more than 200 years of United States history some aspects of mostly shared ideology can be identified and to some extent have prevailed for most of the period. However, there has been change, particularly since the New Deal, in the practical reality of that ideology. Many of the original terms and even beliefs have remained, but their definitions, applications and reality are no longer the same. The core elements of the historical American ideology are:

- Local government
- States rights
- Limited government role
- Taxation with representation
- No government authority or intrusion in the private home or family
- Extensive rights for the individual *citizen*
- Community/social constraint on socio-cultural behavior (independent of or supported by government authority)
- Limited toleration, and control of social misfits

- Representative government - link between government decisions and finance, and election to office
- Military subservient to civilian government
- Male, family and traditional culture-centered, and sexually-conservative social relations
- Dominant middle class culture leadership in social issues with group elites as behavior role models
- European history, English common law and Christian traditions and philosophy
- Full freedom of debate for all as key element of politics and government

The above would be features observed in civics textbooks and held throughout most of American history. However, the reality of these features can now be observed to be quite different as follows:

- National and state regulation, and co-funding in local government, reducing the ambit of local decisions and making local governments increasingly just local implementation agencies
- Federal control over key social, financial, security, education, and insurance subjects, with enforcement of Federal values and standards
- The Federal Reserve and other bureaucratic institutions which introduce regulation and enforcement of regulations without any decision by elected representatives or opportunity for public objection
- Tax-like charges imposed through un-checked regulation
- Government control over extensive social practice and expression
- Limited behavioral control by the community, replaced by behavior control by government and social misfits
- Government as custodian of the home and individuals
- Military as an independent arm of government, as a business and policy tool, and as a part of the bureaucracy
- Open, experimental, individualistic, market-based and non-traditional social relations

- Minority protection and set asides taken from the majority
- No social or cultural development pyramid for behavior role models
- Social theories and multiculturalism guiding identity
- Reduction in the choice of political policy choices and topics of debate

It is clear from the above that the key elements of American traditional ideology are no longer the same and do not represent the traditional middle class ethos. In fact most of these are now the complete opposite – even though many people still assume and support the traditional American ideology. The reality of ideology has changed, but still largely retains positive self-association. This is a result of the words and ways that package and describe the new ideology - also known as propaganda.

There are many detailed and exhaustive books on historical American politics (although sadly they are not hugely popular) that provide insight into slavery, central banking, states' rights, the War of Northern Aggression, etc. From these it can be seen that the key elements of United States history and ideology were relatively clear (although not perfectly so) in the beginning and became more muddled over the next two centuries, and especially since the New Deal and World War II. Many of the changes did not happen overnight, but some actually happened before our very eyes.

There were three stages in the American advantage largely based on the accidental benefits of open space, comparative freedom and continental isolation. These were:

1. windfall land and abundant resources - of greatest benefit to the middle and lower classes
2. development and use of new technology and management - of increasing benefit to the middle and entrepreneur classes
3. the world's reserve currency - of greatest benefit to the financial and management classes

America was able to jump from one stage to another to retain, restore and increase its affluence, and actually improve its social equity. If these stages had been absent, the various social movements such as slavery abolition, women's rights, the labor movement, and social welfare would not have been possible. The same is true for the sexual freedom, children's rights, immigrants rights, affirmative action, diversity programs, etc. that followed. Americans believed that these were political and not economic issues and ultimately were reconciled (or pacified) to accept them largely because they had no *apparent* economic costs, because their social/cultural costs were blindly *ignored* and because there *were* direct economic costs in *fighting* these movements (the Federal Government has largely promoted social activism and reform since the War of Northern Aggression, and opposition could result in jail or employment/business sanctions).

For some time it seemed that all classes and interest groups could benefit continuously. The national myth and social contract were changed to include that erroneous theory - culminating in trickle down and multi-culturalism propaganda. As the resources of the American political economy began to reach their limits, there was no longer a majority middle class with common interests. The middle class had become not the leader, but only one among a number of claimants to benefits from a political economy that is not understood to have any limits. How the middle class became a minority and lost its leadership role and unity are explored in detail in the following chapters.

Chapter 4. The Nature of Reality

Justification Myths

In the previous chapters we saw that the peculiar circumstances of America created unique opportunities to acquire and maintain wealth. As a result middle class justification myths linked with the American ideology developed to promote the self-image of the American people and to satisfy the control interest of the power elite. These myths, explaining "why we have and should enjoy prosperity," originally contained factual components and relationships, which are no longer accurate. Nevertheless, middle class prosperity justification myths remain largely unquestioned. One might wonder how myths with inaccurate causality could be accepted to explain actual experienced conditions.

Here is an example of how the independent truth of two facts can be used to explain a third condition with which they are both independently linked. Living in Pakistan's Northwest Frontier tribal areas are the Pushtun people with a traditional honor-based life code. Some years ago after international mujahideen volunteers were forced to leave Afghanistan, some Arab mujahideen sought refuge and settled in those border areas of Pakistan. After staying for sometime there with nothing to keep them occupied except to observe the local life patterns, the Arabs challenged the Islamic propriety of women working in the fields of one village. A consultative council, "jirga," of senior and influential leaders was held to consider the Arab observation with the decision that: "Pushtuns are Muslim, our tradition is that women work in the fields, so women working in the fields is sanctioned by Islam."

Such simple reasoning sounded amusing at the time, but on reflection I could see that most societies justify their actions and conditions by similar use of identity myth reasoning rather than on direct cause and effect relations. Often outcomes actually generate myths to justify themselves rather than by the myths themselves producing the outcomes. As long as America was prosperous, any justification myth that we adopted could be correct. For example, the myths of democracy, of Christian faith/belief in God, of hard work, of honesty, of being law-abiding - recently of diversity, multiculturalism and equal opportunity - may or may not have been actually true, but we used them to define our motivations and identity. Therefore, any situation we found ourselves in should be a result of those myths. Of course sometimes the situation was not fully to our liking so we could simply say that the cause of that situation was some sort of interference with or short-circuit in the myths rather than a problem with the myths themselves or their causality. In short, believing - and acting on - these American myths required that we remain prosperous, and that no serious analysis of cause and effect be made. Now that we have a permanent decline in American prosperity and other perceived virtues, the myths that explained them and their causality have begun to be questioned.

My principal intention in writing this book was to help me and others, as native-born Americans, to ascertain real conditions in America and their causes. This would seem to be a simple job and we would imagine that much scholarly analysis would be available to achieve this goal. In fact, so much has been written about every aspect of America and American life that I expected that I would only need to consult and sift through that material in order to make an assessment of conditions and causes. The extensive written material and spoken debate about almost aspect of American political economy assumed or accepted traditional, or prevailing conditions as reality and expressed an opinion for or against the conditions *under* that reality. There was a rough consensus of the observed reality. Arguments came from those who didn't like the reality and wanted to change it (normally thought of as revolutionaries or reactionaries), rather than in disputing the reality itself.

The Changed Structure of Discourse

In a short period of time, starting especially in the 1970s the old fashioned structure of debate for or against situations in an accepted reality became muddled and the relativist argument became a world view and gained rapid dominance. The relativist approach was more structural than argumentative. It asserted that the concepts of non-discrimination and self-determination (realization) trumped reality, preferences and any argument, since no correct judgment could be obtained either from analysis of reality or from assessment of outcomes, since they didn't matter in comparison with normative outcomes (what should be rather than what is). Ironically, the relativist position developed into its own absolutist position where there is no free judgment independent of preferred concepts . This illogical and perverse environment where not only opinion of conditions, but also the underlying meaning of conditions themselves are in dispute is suggested by Thomas Sowell in his Vision of the Anointed.

From the relativist approach to debate emerged "trump" (not Donald) judgments which took hold from the 1960s onward. Any expressed judgment, preferential and discriminatory ideas or opinions that could be painted with suddenly-deemed pejorative terms such as prejudice, racism, homophobia and male chauvinism, could easily be dismissed or condemned without the need for argument or justification since these were "not the way things should be". This would allow individuals or opinions to be judged negatively simply by any association with particular terms, whether or not the association was valid or the terms themselves were correct. Instead of being discussed, issues are now classified into terms, and the relationship of those terms with other terms and concepts (such as racism and prejudice, for example) rejecting the standing of any social/cultural preferences and their relationship with the social contract. Thus, there is no right or wrong to be argued for most issues, since many issues have already been defined in the institutional framework of right and wrong *terms*.

In this environment the relativist approach denied that all positions started from an equal status and potential to be held valid since by definition only one side mattered and trumped any other ideas (in the pre-defined classification). It was only necessary to make the connections with key terms to determine right and wrong rather than arguing on individual merits. Where valid arguments could not be denied these were defeated by linkage with Freudian slips, externalizing association or reverse psychology. By introducing the concept that saying one thing and meaning the opposite, and saying something accidentally that was subconsciously intended, any valid argument could be suspect or maligned easily thus eliminating the need to struggle with counter arguments. Using this perverse way of thinking, anyone with a strong opinion against something could actually be for it, and mistakenly saying something unintended would actually be saying what was really intended.

As ridiculous as this seemed as a childish or adolescent game it has gained credence and general usage in daily thinking. This kind of perverse thinking has also been promoted in popular comedy and even seemingly ordinary discourse. Attention to the apparent has gradually shifted to the hidden, which by definition cannot be known. This has increasingly been developed in the advertising industry so that what is important is not how you like the red shirt, but why you bought it and what it means about you. Psychology in general and the Freudian approach in particular have led to the deconstruction of culture by changing its historical references and breaking its social meanings through various twisted and reverse logical arguments. In this environment it is difficult to have any type of debate on a subject since no subject is complete in its apparent character. As a result, contending positions cannot be objectively or internally compared and decided - because they are supposed to have hidden features which are not known.

In today's society there is a lack of objective and argued verification for commonly assumed verities so that just using words, phrases, or concepts acts as a short hand for introducing assumed/unchallenged right and wrong, and for limiting explanation or debate. We have developed a society with an assumptive basis for reasoning, rather than a deduced (objective or subjective) basis of reasoning. This means that we do not talk about good versus evil, or about knowledge versus ignorance, but about what assumptions are supported by sanctioned and approved terms and what positions are for or against those terms. In this environment only those who are empowered to use particular terms have the authority to trump any ideas or concepts not supported by them. We have to ask whether assumptions promoted by the privileged terms are merely based on coincidental association, vague concepts or just on unproven negation of other ideas. As such, argument by terms functions as a sort of unsupported shorthand for making stark definition between the black and white, of inclusion and exclusion, within those terms.

This situation is far removed from the Renaissance and Enlightenment appreciation of truth and investigation. Education in the Post-World War II period began to introduce shibboleths that not only could not be challenged, but that must guide investigation and interpretation. This resulted in a new liberal arts environment where most traditional and historical knowledge and experience were dropped, and where logical, philosophical and experiential judgments were condemned in favor of revolutionary or "progressive" concepts. Wherever a judgment existed, it was to be discarded in favor of a complaint against it since the progressive was by definition the preferred. In the process of converting the liberal arts into social sciences for big government, the importance of philosophical questions about the priorities of man to survive, reproduce, enjoy, achieve and survive was lost.

Revolutionary challenge was the foundation for what has come to be known as so-called "social science" - as if observation of behavior or deduction through philosophy and the classic traditions that had been adequate for all previous human history had suddenly become defunct. Social science assumes a regular distribution of behavior as a system according to some desired or efficiency rules, as opposed to simple observation of individual behavior with respect to cultural, religious or philosophical norms. Once behavior was made a part of a system, every aspect of behavior became worthy of study as an separate element (independent of the whole) in the system. This has resulted in the plethora of topical subjects of study that are now offered in universities. This invention of a this new reality is discussed in detail in World Systems Analysis by Emanuel Wallerstein. The social sciences replaced philosophy, morality and other classical traditions and became the core of American academic and intellectual life which guides education and public discourse and debate, but not personal life. Personal values are still needed to give consistency to any decisions made and paths taken, but cannot be guided by modern social sciences. That is the realm of ethics and judgment which are no longer linked to the broader society by philosophy.

Transition from Morality to Ethics to Economics

Filling the void created by the ascendance of social science, and the decline of religious and community "moral" authority, are associations and activities which give some limited practice guidance (but that have no internal ideological consistency or external authority) such as trade and professional groups. These groups cannot provide moral or philosophical guidance and only serve to guide human energy. Nothing can provide a basis for common values other than common behavior, knowledge and experience. With the loss of religious and community umpires to provide a type of objective judgment and exclude the improper, false and unqualified propositions there is a loss of appreciation for truth and quality since those necessarily require the very value judgment which has been rejected by the relativist debating position.

The resulting current social system exceeds the capacity of individuals to navigate, since an individual's judgment now cannot extend beyond himself. This is especially difficult in a fully individualistic society where all background decisions have to be made over and over again, whereas in a traditional communal society, background decisions are automatic and more efficient within traditional environments. Early stages of individualistic society have some automatic decisions as well as some individual decisions allowing for more adaptability for changing conditions. In our individualistic society the effort required to make all judgments on a personal basis is too great and exceeds the benefits from individual expression and adaptability to changing conditions. As the classic book Propaganda by Edward Bernays notes, under the conditions of modern democratic market society, complete self-direction is impossible so social guidance has to be given through the media. However, since this guidance is not part of any consistent philosophy or ideology, it has to be accepted only on a case by case basis, and provides no reference to other cases.

As a result of this change a greater burden has been placed on ethics. But, ethics is not intended to help identify truth and consistency (the realm of philosophy and to some extent religion and morality), but only to guide proper behavior based on core values. So ethics is useless without shared fundamental understandings - both historical and current - and how they relate to myth and reality. This would suggest the need for religion, philosophy, logic and rhetoric to grow in importance, but the opposite has been true. Religion has been under tremendous attack from all sides for decades and no longer provides independent guidance to society as a whole, but rather reflects elements of the society. Philosophy at least, should be independent of the current social environment, but even philosophy has been cleverly demeaned and distorted through its conversion to economic logic.

Most economics literature structures all human behavior into market relationships that stress increased production/benefits/consumption and do not allow for denial, restriction and meaningful quality distinctions (elitism). In this way the search for truth, which should be guided by philosophy (more precisely aletheia), has been replaced by economics whose job is defining desired or so-called efficient outcomes! In the same manner political economy – the political process of distribution and management of benefits in a society – has also been deceptively integrated into the pseudo-scientific economics to mean the desired mythical market behavior of an efficient society.

Statistics and the New Reality

An important step in advancing this distortion of reality, truth and values is the development and use of statistics. Statistics we are told has its origins in government (state) information. This sounds innocuous enough, but over time statistics has become not just information, but a new discipline in the social sciences. Today statistics has become an all pervasive way of reporting and interpreting reality, substituting for actual experience and perception. Statistics now represents partials rather than quantities. Even in the face of such a fundamental change, there has been no intellectual or philosophical objection. Only a few decades ago information would have been reported and interpreted in terms of numbers such as "1,000 workers laid off" or "price of new Ford to increase by $1,000." Everyone could understand this information since they would imagine the challenge of employing 1,000 workers in alternative jobs or in finding an additional $1,000 to buy a car.

48

Today, statistics largely replaces numbers so that "jobless rate increases by only 0.1 per cent and "car prices to increase by 2.5 per cent.

The transition from simple quantities as the basis for judgment to the use of percentage (the number in every 100), or statistics has further distorted human understanding of reality. Imagine the public reaction if a contagious disease breaks out in elementary schools and is reported as *only* 1 per cent. It would seem to be almost non-existent. But if this is considered as 1 in a 100 students and a school might have 1,000 students, then 10 students would have the disease. Would anyone want their children attending that school? Similarly if people are told that the Hispanic population has reached 13 per cent they might think it is still a relatively small group, but if they read that the Hispanic population is more than 35 million they might wonder how such a large group can be assimilated.

The above examples show how facts, concepts and even disciplines can and have been distorted by disassembly, redefinition, distractions and false images to change visions, goals and behavior in very recent years. This new intellectual environment has supported the substitution of new "politically correct" national myths for previous national myths (based to some extent on previous realities), and the association of these new national myths with national identity, self-image, aspirations and status that are the result of other times and values.

Despite this propagandistic association, however, the collective meaning of the new myths that compose the national ideology is in fact social disunity and opposition to middle class values. The disconnect between the key importance of the traditional middle class social contract and a new national ideology of disunity that has been portrayed as the national (unifying) ideology is the basis for our loss of national social cohesion, virtue and productive dynamism. This makes it urgent for us to review the American ideology and national myths to validate and correct the assumptions and realities that they claim to represent.

We have seen how the substitution of new myths in the American ideology and contemporary methods of debate broke down the basis for the middle class social contract and understanding of history in the United States. In the following chapters we will see how it was possible for modern America to reinvent itself under this new social "construct" without a social "contract". Post-World War II prosperity and the establishment of the American Empire hid and pacified most ideological and social conflicts for a time, but as the conflicts became too great to be sustained by the declining national wealth and common values, American society has been splintered into many factions competing for limited resources in the political economy.

Chapter 5. Divide and Conquer

The Change in American Ideology

In earlier chapters we have seen that the basis for discourse, and even thinking, in the United States changed fundamentally, but what caused the earlier American ideology to change so fundamentally over such a short period of time without a huge debate? To a considerable extent the lack of debate was due to the fundamental dislocation of thought and discourse. And of course there was deep political discord surrounding many issues such as the Civil Rights Movement and the follow on women's, sexual, immigrant, diversity, self-expression and the less discussed elite/technical/financial empowerment movements. However the issues raised in these movements focused mainly on the political framework and not on the nature of the society as defined in the myth-based American ideology. Over a short period of time Americans began to think that political changes did not affect non-political society, and paid limited attention and resistance to the aftermath of political changes.

Nevertheless, changes that came about though the political system automatically seeped into the American ideology so that it began to be understood that the current American society was the very same as that which built the nation and provided its social contract. The reason for the largely un-protested change in the American ideology is that the disruptive political movements mentioned above appeared mainly as a result of temporary and unnatural world economic and political conditions and cannot be justified or sustained in the United States or other countries as world conditions rebalance. In order to explore this assertion we should consider the nature of the temporary and unnatural world economic and political conditions that engendered those political movements.

We should understand that United States history was largely based on the incidental benefits of open space, comparative freedom and continental isolation. We can say that these determined the fundamental nature of America. The first two stages of American history were directly related to these benefits: 1. reaping benefits of windfall land and abundant resources, and 2. development and use of new technology and management organization. The third stage is the very recent Post-World War II American history with the establishment of the world's reserve currency, American Empire and globalization. It could be suggested that we are now entering a fourth stage of mass population manipulation and control, but that should be explored elsewhere.

The Loss of the Social Contract and the Transition to Statism

In one scene from a movie about John Adams, a leader of the American Revolution, in response to the issue of the "rights of Englishmen," one official said, "the Crown has ordered and the only course is obedience; you would do well to accept that and act accordingly". The official meant that it was Crown that decided what those rights were. Colonial Americans argued that the law was used to crush their rights, but the British Crown did not consider Colonial interests as rights and so used the law to deny them. Both positions were justified, but there was only one state (the Crown) and its supporters were the controlling power, so they defined the nature of Colonial rights. It was necessary to have a War of Independence in order to break the control over the part of the state that was the American Colonies. Once that was done the new American Government could define the rights of its citizens according to its own concepts. The lessons to be drawn from this episode are that interests are not rights, and that it is the state power that defines any rights.

Much American policy debate in recent years has focused on making group interests into rights and entitlements, but this process of political transition from interests and entitlements to rights has been largely ignored by the general public. One of the core issues in the debate was that of the dominant culture (the state) somehow being responsible for the lack of success or disabilities of other groups. Of course this is to some extent true by its very dominance. The general nature of society is that the dominant culture enjoys a larger share of its benefits. In the United States for most of its history, *the values and interests of the dominant middle class culture were expressed and reinforced by its laws*. The unique feature of American society was that subordinate cultures were also granted considerable benefits - but these benefits were special *"consideration" rather than rights*.

Normally this inequitable situation is accepted, although it is not liked by all. However, in the United States starting with the Whiskey Rebellion and continuing through the War of Northern Aggression, statist government re-emerged from the euphoria of Independence and re-established/redefined dominant American values and interests generally less onerous and restrictive than in the latter Colonial period, but without substantially altering the power of the state to define rights, and to enforce dominant values and interests through law and executive orders.

However, there was a remarkable lack of conflict in core interests between the power elite and the middle class, which together formed the dominant culture, due in large part to the excess of resources. Whenever there was an economic conflict of interest state power and law was usually used to decide in favor of the power elite. In the case of cultural values, the state and the law largely accepted the middle class culture as its unwritten guidance. The state and laws did not always actively promote the dominant culture, but they did not prevent the community itself from enforcing its values in whatever manner necessary. State power and the law did not *define* national values, but *promoted and ensured* the dominant cultural values.

In the larger historical context there were often two political opinions with one having a larger following or greater power support. The opinion of the majority or the powerful always won. However, the United States Government was developed mostly by individuals who had at some time or place been members of some sort of minority and who sought to provide majority rule with some protection for minorities, and the exercise of judgment in implementation and debate of issues. This was never meant to negate the rule of the majority, however that was defined, only that particular minorities might be given some opportunity for public expression and private behavior. This opportunity for expression was never intended for all minorities, all public expression or even all private behavior, only those within the tolerance range of the dominant culture. It certainly never meant equality in government or society for all individuals or groups; only opportunity for an acceptable range of ideas and private behavior.

Over time and carrying forward the experience of British political economy, state power and the law in the United States assumed the primary responsibility of enforcing unwritten values so that informal social and community action was not much needed for this task. In short the community gave up its active role and duty in ensuring social order on the assumption that the state and law would do this. For generations this combined formal and informal system appeared to work well because a social contract recognized dominant concepts and values.

Those misfits not sharing the dominant culture's concepts and values either had to accept a subordinate status or relocate (physically or functionally) where there was some degree of autonomy for alternate values. This actually took place over time along with other changes such as urbanization and the technological revolution. As a result, misfits gradually began to become powerful in fulcrum locations such as cities and in professions such as communications and entertainment that did not require close co-existence with the dominant culture. As American society continued to be further politically dissected, and to be diluted through immigration a point was reached where the dominant concepts and values began to be challenged.

This presented a huge challenge to the political/legal system since the underlying concepts and values were not written and codified, but were like the English Common Law, largely assumed based on common experience and use. As a result of challenges to the dominant culture, the law began to assert its own judgment independent of historical precedent. It was in this light that Solzhenitsyn wrote that the United States had become a legalistic instead of moral society. As a result, at some time starting especially in the 1960s, the law separated from the values of the dominant culture and what they considered right, further promoting divergence from common values. As a result, many issues, even minor ones, developed lives of their own to be resolved through technical legal machinations, extra-legal administrative procedures or public agitation.

Since law no longer had its base in the historical social contract, it could be changed, or even interpreted more or less freely; something that it had never had preparation or occasion to do. Being dislodged from the middle class social contract, the law and other tools could only be used by the power elite and those outside of the social contract, which ultimately meant the state. If the law remained only for the use and benefit of the state and its interests, rather than to enforce the social contract, then the American State became justified to use the law to reduce influence of the middle class and suppress those who would defy the power elite.

Carrying this dramatic change further into implementation, since the law is only for the benefit of the state, there is now for the first time in American history a dispute not only as to what the law means, but also as to whether it should actually be enforced, particularly in the case of immigration and federal-state powers. Since enforcement of the law has become discretionary, vestiges of the law that do not support the state interests can be discarded through court interpretation or even directly ignored. There are too many examples of this current practice to give here. The entitled, rich, famous, influential and victim-status claimants are able to avoid punishment on technicalities and lack of action by the state. At the same time, ordinary people are harassed often with the knowledge that they are unable to fight for their acknowledged rights. In this environment the state does not serve the society, but seeks to create a society to suit its political economic ambitions.

American Exceptionalism or Myopia

Although many social, political and economic trends were under way in the United States even from its earliest days, the pace of development and change increased in the 20th Century and especially after World War II. The United States did not suffer nearly to the same extent as Europe and Asia from the destruction of the War, but World War II brought its own disruption in the United States. This was in the form of massive dislocation to urban areas from rural areas and small towns, a shift from own-account business and labor to wage employment, and a disruption and consequent mixing of social groups unprecedented in human history.

This was accompanied by a parallel unprecedented explosion of new technology and consumer affluence, largely based on the unique position of the United States as the world's hegemonistic industrial and financial power. Together these conditions resulted in a social and cultural vacuum, intoxication and confusion as people sought to assess their identity and the meaning of life. In this vacuum literally everything was thrown open for debate - and, unique in history - without any apparent or acknowledged negative economic or social consequences. Almost all changes from tradition were seen as just increases in the total social welfare.

At the same time a cultural myopia came to be characteristic of American, and to some extent of European societies in the Post-World War II period. What was this myopia? Often Americans are accused of being cocooned in their own experience and not open to other cultures. This is another subject altogether, but I should note that this is in itself a certain type of propaganda which distorts actual reality. There is a fundamental difference between this excessively self-confident or self-centered character, and the myopia that I am suggesting.

This myopia is the view of the world structure that prevailed after World War II; namely, a world divided broadly into the First, Second and Third World; with the second being the core communist block countries. The nature of the Cold War virtually froze all these groups in place with limited interaction except for various military operations, espionage, limited immigration to address labor shortages and technical assistance to the third world. Of course, each of these elements of limited interaction would create unanticipated conditions of its own, but those conditions came to have broader significance at later times. Until 30-40 years after World War II this "frozen" international structure was combined with extensive economic and technical expansion in the First World, especially the United States. The result was that most of the American day to day system and public was almost completely isolated from much of the world. It was as if the Second and Third worlds were on another planet. That meant that the only world that mattered was our own First World. In that framework our actions were the world - our world - and the actions of others either didn't matter or were the desired responses to our own actions and contained within their world.

When we read the books, listen to music and watch movies from the Post-World War II period it is clear that from conservative ideologues to utopian visionaries to social reformers and finally to the self-absorbed hippie generation, nearly all Americans were basing their world view and plans on the assumption that their ideas really mattered, that their ideas were only in competition with their domestic opponents, that there was no significant cost to their ideas and that if they prevailed the results would be as they wished. Even the great peaceniks and one-worlders assumed that they were the prime movers and that there would be world peace and brotherhood only as a result of their ideas and efforts. As it turns out, this was not a true understanding of the world situation. It was the special cocoon view of a special period. Once that period ended, all those assumptions would have to be dropped and Americans would have to become just other people living in the world without any special privilege except for their geographic location and history. Yet, even as this world situation has changed, most Americans have not responded in a reasonable way. Even in the midst of this cataclysmic change the new idea of American Exceptionalism has emerged adding to the cacophony of the fiddling while Rome (America) burns.

The next chapters give examples of how trends and events in the second half of the 20th Century led to the breakdown of the social contract into conflicting group politics, and ultimately in the surrender of social control by the dominant middle class culture to the state and power elites.

Chapter 6. The Civil Rights Movement

The Civil Rights Movement (CRM) was a complicated mix of history, culture and issues. Its name provided a good description of its origin and objectives which were fairly simple. The process of attaining those objectives was not so simple. As the words "civil rights" imply, the struggle was for rights of the people that were believed to be provided by the constitution, but were denied by implementation or cultural processes. Of course, seen in this way, this was anything but simple since the devil is always in the details. For example, was the CRM primarily interested in integrated common schools, equal government support of civic amenities, or the removal of egregious disabilities and injustice (such as public place and business segregation, lynching and unrepresentative legal procedures), was it concerned with the aggressive uplifting of African-American society or was it a actually a deeper cultural struggle to assert new values and behavior over the majority white community? The CRM started out as a battle for initiation, extension, restoration or restitution of assumed rights under the constitution – but where did it end?

At the time of the CRM a white middle class culture prevailed in the United States, even in parts of the African-American community. Excessive dominance was possible especially from the lower end of the white cultural spectrum. That was in consonance with normal historical human experience. Some groups do better in any society. But some African-Americans were also winners in the American society. The white community was inclusive to some extent even as it maintained its overall hegemony and coherence, ultimately guiding the African-American community toward a sort of ultimate convergence with the white culture in the same way that the Indian caste system allows non-caste communities to enter the caste system and even some castes to change their position within the overall framework. Of course there are always those at the bottom and in America they were frequently, but not always African-Americans. Poor whites and some mixed race groups could generally ensure that they stayed off the bottom by virtue of their tenuous link to higher white culture.

The so-called CRM had a special focus on the particular social structure in the South which was semi-agrarian, but urbanizing, and ultimately unsustainable. The objective of the CRM may have been less for fair treatment and respect, although most of its supporters probably thought that was the objective, than it was for access to resources and opportunities such as education, and to advancement within an ever expanding economic pie. Ironically, the CRM emerged during a narrow time window when the access to and opportunities themselves could be expanded with little apparent cost due to the unique short term Post-World War II prosperity in the United States. As a result it appeared that new people, African-Americans, could be given new opportunities, additional to the existing opportunities, which would not harm the current position of whites. There was very little debate about this point, because of the false assumption that the short term economic prosperity was a natural consequence of the American "system" and could be sustained and increased indefinitely. As a result there was no debate on the cost of the CRM, but rather on the social and political needs and foreseen impacts. Specifically, there was debate on whether white culture would continue to be dominant, whether the white-dominated system could include racial preference and whether any behavior could be a criterion for inclusion or access.

Obviously, the overwhelming white majority that controlled all institutions in the United States would never have accepted the CRM without a blood bath if it thought its position of privilege would be significantly harmed. Instead, it was ultimately suggested that there was an ever-expanding pie of access and benefits and that more of these could be given to African-Americans without harm to the white position. At the beginning of the CRM African-Americans had a commonly shared reality: blacks faced discrimination which limited their access to the ever-expanding pie.

One group of whites thought that there was a justification for the discrimination. A second group believed that fundamentally there was no meaningful difference between African-Americans and whites, but only the so-called white prejudice, and that African-American culture would not be any more substantially different from an average white American culture than various white minority cultures once discrimination was removed. Even though there were superficial cultural differences, these would have no different economic/functional value, and there was no justification for "discrimination" other than to prevent African-Americans from having a competing voice in the national society.

A third group emerged that felt that there could be no justification for discrimination even where there were clear differences, because *values and preferences* "didn't matter." The "didn't matter" or relativist group was not seen to be particularly separate or threatening at that time, but ultimately evolved into a key force in the youth movement of the 1960s and the predominant "liberal" social, political and business paradigm of current times. This has often been taken a step further by even preferring the so-called "African-American culture" or other "non-white cultures" over the "white" culture by both African-Americans and whites.

The thinking of the latter two groups was related to the American and Enlightenment myths of human development which found their ultimate Waterloo in Francis Fukuyama's The End of History. According to these myths, ultimately history and traditional culture had no meaning and all human development would have a common result. In this vision mainly held by those of higher socioeconomic status, African-Americans and whites would just be Americans of different colors. This is a complicated subject to which we will return later. Fundamentally this meant that discrimination was bad mainly because it wasted energy and talent. While there could be a different African-American culture, it would really be just a private persona such as a hair style and would not meaningfully affect public performance in the economic or governance systems, since the ultimate and fundamental nature of people, especially Americans, was efficient, productive and satisfied by consumption.

Moreover, differences in culture would have no normative meaning and should not be used in judging "rights," opportunities or access. Obviously, this issue would have the most relevance to the lower strata of white society since the value of their cultural inheritance was comparatively more than for those of higher status. If this inheritance were rendered of no value, which is ultimately what equal cultural value means in our competitive society, whites from the lower socioeconomic groups, would lose out. That is exactly what happened, with far reaching consequences beyond the CRM and its relation to African-Americans. Ultimately, those from higher socioeconomic groups could segregate themselves from other cultural groups by virtue of their economic performance, while those in lower socioeconomic groups would have to compete on a level playing field on a continuous cultural and economic basis. This raises the question of whether there is any lasting culture without economic and political power, or at least physical segregation.

It is curious that whites from the middle and lower socioeconomic strata have not been able to defend their positions. It may be due to the lack of leadership from within their own ranks, the total betrayal of them by the upper socioeconomic classes, or to their own buying into the argument that culture doesn't matter in economic (or political) life. Whatever the reason, the success of the CRM could not have been due to a willing cultural suicide, and the arguments for the CRM and its expected results must have been considered politically and economically possible to accommodate independent of any rights-based justification. How could this be?

The underlying myth (theory) supporting this was that the economy could sustain the increased costs for civil rights opportunities because it had excess wealth and unlimited potential. But, in fact, the United States economy had already peaked with respect to price competitiveness, and the costs of civil rights benefits would necessarily have a negative effect on the economy unless they were absorbed by overall economic growth. There was definitely economic and job growth from the 1960s until the recent recession in 2008. However, production employment declined precipitously. The growth areas were mainly in government, technology, education, low level service sector, sales, finance and related support fields, which are less beneficial and sometimes extractive sectors.

The result of the CRM was that due to affirmative action and legal conflict mitigation policies, clever and ambitious African-Americans found employment that was additional to that which would have been available in the absence of the CRM. In those cases as well as where existing jobs rather than additional ones were filled by African-Americans, the standards were almost universally lowered to provide special opportunities.

A major contribution to African-American opportunities was the growth of the government sector. It appears that a much larger part of government employment from expansion or reallocation than of private sector employment was given to African-Americans. Over time the private sector appears to have been won over to providing more jobs to African-Americans, and it is not clear whether the lowered resistance to affirmative action in the private sector is due to profit derived from business with government, to increased market opportunities in the African-American community, or actual belief in any performance or political justification. Of course, in some cases the private sector also cleverly managed to reduce the affirmative action quota of African-Americans, by hiring women, so-called Hispanics and persons from other groups, including immigrants, who were generally more efficient and needed less help - or none at all.

African-American culture provided historical elements of jazz and soul food, but nothing much else until the CRM "liberation" when it introduced African-American basketball, soul and dance music, rap music, ghetto culture, drug dealing, common fatherless households, etc. Although some African-Americans have adopted the middle class culture and achieved in it, this has not really meant much to the broader African-American community which has only achieved freedom as a result of its culture being merged with a sinking white culture. This is something like what George Wallace and other segregationists claimed would happen, but all the elites and bleeding hearts refused to believe it. Wallace and the others were mostly correct, but American society had changed so fundamentally that it the effect was more complicated and even it no longer mattered. The CRM was peacefully accepted and moved ahead because it was assumed that elevating African-Americans would not lower whites, but it did, and no one cared – not even George Wallace!

The other main area of new employment for African-Americans was in entertainment. Entertainment includes sports, music – and also politics and drugs. As the barriers to African-American participation in these sectors fell, African-American participation increased, but white participation also decreased. This is especially noticeable in sports such as basketball and popular music. Moreover, this took place at a time when entertainment was gaining a larger and stronger importance in American society and the world as traditional culture declined. As a result this also gave African-Americans the opportunity to gain status and influence through the back door. To the extent that entertainment figures did not self destruct, their offspring might expect to enter well-known schools and/or pursue employment as second generation entertainers. The related subject of the creation of such new occupational and technology castes requires separate attention.

It might also be noted that in addition to African-Americans themselves, mainly middle class, the other proponents of equal rights and affirmation action were to a large extent, bleeding heart whites. One could ask, why this would be the case. The motivation of bleeding hearts can probably be traced to the anti-slavery movement in England, and later through its political and economic manifestations leading up to and in relation to the War of Northern Aggression. The British and the northern United States economies had only nominal economic relations with slave labor-based agriculture by the mid-19th Century and that allowed them to develop an aversion to, what was historically a well established practice and social structure.

During and after the CRM the bleeding heart whites, initially in the North and later in the South itself, began to find fault with all manner of discrimination against African-Americans and later to adopt a common vocabulary of complaint. Their political interference in the South - and also in some other places such as Boston – shows the modern manifestation of a long-running self-righteousness to which there is no limit in the United States. In recent years the targets of this self-righteousness have been extended throughout the world even to Russia and traditional societies such as Afghanistan. Despite the rhetoric supporting self-determination, democracy and traditional values, these are only accepted and supported if they do not conflict with self-righteous so-called "progressive", social power and economic interests.

The inclusion of Southern Whites in the CRM can be seen as a result of a Northern population influx into the South, transition from regional to national cultural expression and media presentation, and an expansion of the population that did not have any direct relation with African-Americans and could pursue a privately (as opposed to publicly) segregated lifestyle.

The role of Jews in the CRM is well known. African-Americans were not well represented in Southern factory labor related to Jewish businesses, and the purely rural economy was largely under the control of white Christians. It was the small town, and urban businesses and professions where Jews had some presence and had some business relations with African-Americans. So, in general there would be no major social or economic conflicts between Jews and African-Americans, unlike the situation with many Christian whites, particularly from the working classes. Still, Southern Jews were probably not very active in the CRM. It was Northern Jews who took up positions as advisors to the CRM, such as with the ACLU and SPLC, and also as less permanent volunteers (again to be seen in the 2008 Presidential Election).

The End of Public Discrimination

Initially it appeared as if the CRM was only for African-Americans and also for "justice," as if justice had some independent and absolute affordability. However, the more fundamental issue was the extent to which American society could continue to structure itself with a preference for the majority over the minority. There are always members of society that suffer from natural, social or cultural conditions. Free choice and limited resources create situations where there are winners and losers. Winners may choose to support losers independently of the social system. However, since this charity is voluntary, the losers will always be in a disadvantaged situation and will often suffer. The CRM began the process of introducing entitlements that are not just protection from active harm, but also claims on involuntary support from the political economy.

The impact of this cannot be overemphasized. If the result of the CRM had only been greater protection to African-Americans in their routine personal lives the result would have been less revolutionary.

However, instead the final result was that job hiring could not be based on the free choice of the employer. More seriously this meant that personal preference moved into the public domain and could be regulated. To the extent that personal preference is found to be socially determined, social preference could also be regulated (this can also be seen by the recent redefinition of some acts as "hate crimes" as distinct from "ordinary" crimes and of other expressions of preference such as "racism, sexism, and various "phobias" when they can be related to groups of people, but not to the fundamental characteristics of the acts themselves. Regulation of preference in social and business environments is a form of totalitarianism, by proposing that all persons have equal rights to all aspects of society, including status, and not just rights under the law. This precludes individual preferences and individual discrimination based on personal characteristics, since ultimately there is nothing in society but individuals and individual behavior (even government is not a separate identity from the individuals that make it up).

An unintended consequence of the CRM is that once individual (and social) preferences were disqualified in principle, it was not only African-Americans who could claim a universal entitlement; all could. Equal participation in any activity then became an entitlement or right whether or not it is reasonable, affordable, or whether other participants or organizers wish it or not (a good example is handicapped access to virtually all activities despite the cost). The impact of the CRM meant that "public" discrimination was not acceptable in American society, regardless of its basis, justification, or its link with individual freedom. In this situation "rights" trumped "freedom." But how is public discrimination different than private discrimination? After the CRM social revolution, it was only a matter of implementation and time before the public and private realms were combined, since it is difficult to have significant private values, behavior and preferences that are not translated into the public sphere. Or is it?

Prior to the CRM there was a public consensus on some general principles that allowed public, social and informal control which both encouraged and discouraged ideas, activities and behavior. The majority of the population, especially outside of large urban areas, extended its personal ethos to the public sphere, and in doing so, largely dismantled its insular family and personal protection walls, often still found among minority groups, in favor of public walls. This was largely the beauty of the "small town America" or community America that Alexis de Tocqueville in ±and later Martin Marty in <u>Pilgrims in their Own Land</u> wrote about. Instead of having to live as only families against the world, so to speak, community Americans used the power of their social institutions and government to protect their personal values. Generally, outside of large urban areas, this provided great efficiency in society. Some groups, notably Catholics, mainly in urban areas, found additional separate organizations necessary to support common values, but this declined over time. As a result, majority preferences were exercised both informally and through public institutions. However, private discriminatory organizations at the community level were not of so much direct social consequence and largely supported the general consensus enforced through public institutions.

When the CRM broke the back of this system, all public institutions and activities came within the purview of anti-discrimination efforts on behalf of African-Americans and later other grievance groups. By their very nature African-Americans and other minorities were organized with a common grievance; i.e. being excluded from the dominant majority. The CRM happened at a time of significant changes in many spheres of life so that the ramifications of the entire process could not be thought through. The CRM forced the majority community to surrender its public personal social protection although there was no mass participation private personal structure to replace it. While African-Americans demanded entrance and equal participation (not only access) to the public system, they continued to maintain their own well developed private group identity. Few whites would seek to join private African-American groups, but the most important white majority groups were in the public sphere and the benefits of these were valued by grievance groups.

The result was that, after some isolated resistance from the likes of George Wallace, the elite white leadership largely sought accommodation with African-Americans in the public sphere and ceased to provide leadership for the majority community where a public consensus had previously existed, as it comfortably retreated into its own private elite institutions. The larger white community either had to ape their former leaders and shed their values and preferences except in the home, or put up vain cultural resistance through lower level and desperate activities (often identified as redneck behavior). These two streams had become quite distinct in the 1960s, but the lower status mass group declined from the 1970s onward due to the lack of any meaningful group leadership. Ultimately most whites are not, or are no longer, suited to intensive private and personal cultural behavior, so they must follow the patterns of the larger society, especially in the age of mass communications and marketing.

As a result, we find the more successful elite group forgetting or diluting their own cultural heritage publicly (wishing people Happy Holidays for example instead of Merry Christmas, and referring to Judeo-Christian values instead of possible specific common or separate Christian and Jewish values) and gradually losing its meaningful culture even in the private sphere (the full effect of this has started to be noticed in the recent X, Y, Millennial or whatever generations when they lose their economic capacity to buy lost culture). The less successful mass majority group has been increasingly drawn to a lower level experiential culture in the face of the loss of leadership. As a result we find the previously most anti-

African-American, anti-drug and self-reliant class to be perversely attracted to the ideas and behavior that it was formerly opposed to - because of its lack of functional alternatives.

Affirmative action meant that less qualification was required which further increased the costs and reduced the level of performance. As noted earlier, this additional cost was initially not a problem when there were no competing international producers, but when foreign, producers, and alternative behavior or technology (suburbanization, consulting, telecommuting, outsourcing, off-shoring, automation) became available, these additional costs resulted not only in reduced consumption of domestic products, but also often in outright substitution of foreign products and services. At the same time the value-free marketing and communications ethics and economics further isolated public life from community and personal values.

More and more people began to consider all life except personal and mainly private matters to be free of traditional values. In that environment one could cease trading with a local hardware store operated by a neighbor in favor of trade with Walmart on the premise that economics and business are value-free and efficient. One exception to this is the action on the part of a small group to voluntarily trade with vendors that support trendy issues like preservation of the rainforest. However, such voluntary political statements are not the same as structural support to a community value-based economic system, which largely prevailed before the 1970s (reference changes in distribution rules at that time that brought more competition, less local ownership and lower prices).

Social and Political Affordability of the CRM

One might ask how the livelihoods of whites were affected by the CRM, and who did the jobs left by African-Americans. A change began to be felt in many ways in the late 1960s and in the 1970s. By 1980 when Ronald Reagan was elected President, the United States economy was in a bad state, due in large part to the CRM and associated disturbances. Many of the white jobs in the Rust Belt simply disappeared. At that time further destruction should have been expected to the economy, but instead there appeared to be a turnaround and improvement in many broad indicators such as employment that had been negatively affected by the CRM and other trends that reduced American competitiveness. As a result, the broad negative impact on white livelihood appeared to be short lived, not deep and so did not provoke white civil unrest.

The United States began to see significant migration to areas where there were jobs, and the computer and Internet revolutions provided new jobs in many places, but most of these were not of the same standard as previous factory work. This was also a period of unprecedented immigration which created much service sector economic activity that provided employment to whites who normally would have worked in manufacturing or in the government jobs that began to be assigned to African-Americans. However, this was not an even trade, since more and more families needed two incomes to make ends meet even with reduced family sizes. Many whites were moderately successful in this interim economy as commission agents (distributors, sales representatives, etc.) rather than as producers (who were increasingly located overseas). This economy depended on consumption and growth, rather than production and concrete value addition. As long as this consumption and growth continued there seemed to be no extreme harmful economic effects from the traumatic social upheaval of the 1960s and 1970s.

Unfortunately, this was a chimera primarily due to immigration and the United States Dollar as a reserve currency (making actual production to generate wealth almost unnecessary!). It should also be noted that during the Post-World War II era Americans moved from self-sufficient farms and rural homesteads to suburbs and metropolitan areas where there was no self-sufficiency and everything had to be bought on a continuous basis. So, where previous generations had owned land and farmhouses as a form of savings security, America's Post-World War II generations have high mortgages on suburban houses with no productive land or buffer savings (even soil for gardening has to be bought) so that nearly all their current income comes from immediate money transfers and is committed on a monthly basis for their lifetimes.

The immediate substitution for this loss of self-sufficiency and buffer security was the dramatic increase in consumption of conveniences and a comparative increase in urban property values. As the durability of conveniences declined (planned obsolescence) capital accumulation was reduced (for example a 1950s refrigerator or washing machine might have an unlimited use life, but once it was replaced with a modern machine from the 1980s onward, a cycle of continuous replacement and capital loss would begin). Moreover, the housing bubble in the first decade of the 21st Century revealed the loss of relationship between investment and productive use in property values. Ultimately the increase of price cannot justify itself in the absence of use value.

Conclusion

Looking at the CRM in an isolated and clinical way decades later to some extent allows a more balanced assessment than was possible at the time. For example, how did the CRM morph into an anti-middle class cultural movement? First of all it employed new battle terms and new definitions of old terms such as racism, discrimination, prejudice (I once heard someone say that prejudice against prejudice is still prejudice).

African-Americans were considerably restricted from access to benefits like education and the resulting success and wellbeing (as if there really was an Adam Smith ever expanding pie). Initially the argument was made that this restriction should be removed (an argument not necessarily valid, but reasonable). When restrictions to their equal access were removed it was seen that African-Americans often did not meet the standards, affirmative action programs were developed to in effect suspend or change the standard itself. The result was that reserved positions were created to include and use African-Americans at any standard that they might present. As a result, universities, government and business have become more demographically representative because of the suspension and sometimes removal of standards.

What was ignored after the once public harassment of African-Americans ended was the need for a framework of mutually respecting yet mutually exclusive cultural spheres. This could not be achieved because the real struggle was actually over *dominant* middle class cultural values and not really over *oppression* which was perhaps one manifestation of those dominant values. The result has been the replacement of personal identity and integrity by superficial apologism, by ignoring the authentic natures of different cultures, and denying preferences and prejudice as fundamental rights and free speech. This prevents essential communication from one authentic cultural and individual identity to another, and destroys the meaningful (if not always pleasant) human relationships that are ultimately necessary for any individual or society.

Chapter 7. Women's Rights Movement

Overview

The CRM pattern was replicated in the women's rights movement (WRM) and the more radical women's liberation movement (WLM). Like the CRM, the WRM initially made a claim for equal political rights. The WRM secondarily strove for behavioral and occupational freedom *within the general social norms*. It should be noted that some women (and other special rights claimants as well) in the 19th and 20th Centuries were able to gain education and do jobs, but that they were generally constrained by the social system within a narrow range of opportunities. The WRM initially began with the premise that women were not given equal opportunity in the universal social framework beginning with the right to vote. However, once the right to vote was achieved there were still other legal issues to be resolved to allow women full independence. Even so, some women did not face insurmountable problems within the otherwise restrictive society.

However, over time the broader, and more radical, WLM ultimately was concerned with changing social attitudes toward the role of women as homemakers and mothers. The core idea, at least of the radicals, was that women should be able to live and work the same way as men, and to obtain the education to do this. Although not articulated or perceived at the time, this would ultimately mean the changing of the social structure itself. Reform or revolutionary movements originate within the existing environment that they wish to change and rarely understand how much change is possible within the broad existing structure before the structure is changed itself and along with it the original framework for the movement.

Of course, on the face of it full freedom and equality with men is totally absurd because the social demand on women for homemaking

74

and mothering is too great to allow more than a small minority of women to participate in any opening up of new opportunities; probably about the same number of unique and uniquely talented women who had done so in the past without special consideration. Women may be extremely capable, but few are so amazing that they can perform salaried work as well as home responsibilities. Yet, Americans bought into this idea and have integrated it into their national ideology, as a result of the brief unprecedented prosperity and freedom from historical human resource constraints.

When considering the modern urbanization of the population, increase in workforce participation and time wasted in commuting, it is clear that some time and labor substitutes for housewives would have to be provided in order to sustain the family structure and its members. This was initially done through day care and expanded primary education for children. It was continued with the introduction of labor and time saving equipment, and the reduction of personal and community activities. For the more affluent, immigration allowed the use of home child care and home-making staff that had been mostly lost as a result of the CRM. However, this substitute labor force was not the social equal of the natural family structure, and largely treated the immigrants and the work of home-making as less important than other activities. The result has been as expected; declining standards of behavior, weakened understanding of tradition and place, a la carte relationships, etc.

The WLM in the 1960s was more far reaching than the WRM, and the CRM, because of its objective of changing fundamental social structures and not just preferences. This movement was particularly focused on the issue and structure of childbearing; closely related to morality and sexual behavior. The basic issue promoted by the movement was that women should be able to live without concern for childbearing. Previously this had meant abstinence from sex or lesbianism. Now the objective was for women to have sexual and social freedom by being liberated from the possibility of child bearing itself. That is really what it was; liberation from child bearing. Yet, child bearing is the cornerstone of a society so no sane person should broadly support such an idea. So how could this idea have progressed and the related unnatural lifestyle become an accepted part of the social structure? Ultimately it comes down to the illusion that the current generation was so special and affluent that it could be detached from both past behavior and future needs.

The idea that women should have the same freedom as men in sexual behavior may sound a little reasonable at first reading, but quickly this is revealed to be a mistake. It assumes first that men actually had sexual freedom and then that matching that freedom with a parallel freedom for women would be a positive contribution to society. The first stage results of the WLM were increased promiscuity among both men and women, increased age at marriage and childbearing, reduction in the number of children born (especially to married couples), introduction of temporary relationships and experiences substituting for marriage or courtship, and changes in relationships between parents and children due to age differences (yet to be fully examined).

The vast majority of women have now adopted non-traditional lifestyles which has resulted in a majority of working women who are poorly able to afford child support; and the explosion in the number of illegitimate children (now often defined non judgmentally as children of single parents), the cost of both which must be to some extent now be supported by the broad society. The second stage results of the WLM were the idea of a "new man" and new concepts of roles for men and women. Basically this meant that gender should not be a factor in determining individual behavior and values, in much the same way as race should not be. Beyond denying reality, this meant further dilution of male employment opportunities, and reduced cultural preservation, family control, and reproduction of the species.

What was the gain from the WRM other than a great increase in the work force participation of ordinary humans? In fact we may find that if a full cost accounting is made society may be found to be much worse off as a result of the WRM. Despite the popular notion to the contrary; one person's gain is another's loss. It should be noted here that in the early days of the WRM it was strenuously denied that women would ever do the heavy labor jobs that men did, such as combat in the military. Of course, like other once controversial issues, this too has been conveniently forgotten and even repudiated as a result of the one foot in the door clause. The increased universal formal work force involvement of women, and the direct competition between men and women is without historical precedent. What is the purpose of this? Is it to rework society for improved self-realization, to serve some theoretical economic argument of labor force efficiency, or to merely to break down the family and social unity?

At the same time as gender has been promoted to be of no importance - unless it is an advantage to women such as in the role of spokesman for sensitive issues - a contradictory new myth is being developed that both women and children are somehow innocent, vulnerable and righteous, and deserve special attention. This special attention required would not normally be given under a traditional social structure since the family as a unit would be the priority of society, but the broad population class of women and children now requires special attention independent from that of the family unit, and new resources from those who don't need that special attention. Now that masculine work and life is demeaned and neutered, disempowered men are conveniently ignored while empowered women and children get special help. Who will provide this special attention - the men who have shed their masculinity and taken up office jobs? Perhaps the career women who have forsaken traditional lives? The WRM social revolution has resulted in new employment opportunities for those who can adjust to the changed social environment, but requires them to pay for the greater number of those who can't adjust through government transfers and negative social impacts. Based on actual results rather than supporting arguments, the WRM should ultimately be seen as a family and men's disempowerment movement.

Chapter 8. Revolution in the Family

Birth Control and Heterosexual Freedom

Artificial birth control has become so ubiquitous that one hardly even gives it a second thought nowadays. However, an overview of its key elements would be helpful in understanding its impact and affect on modern lives. The traditional birth control method was physical abstinence or any other method which could prevent sharing of fertility between male and female partners. Artificial birth control really got its start with the condom, which has been around for a few generations, but is of comparatively recent near-universal availability. At the time of its introduction it was seen as only a convenience tool to assist with lifestyle scheduling and avoiding social relationship complications. However, as other social barriers dropped, the condom came to be used more broadly it began to provide freedom generally from the procreation consequences of natural human life cycle urges and physical needs. As a result, natural family creation patterns were gradually disturbed in order to accommodate the management and freedom desires of modern life.

Other methods of birth control, especially the birth control pill have provided further opportunity for sex without procreation. The birth control pill basically disturbs the female hormonal system so that it does not react to male fertility with conception. It is almost certain that this will have more health and behavioral effects than are currently understood. For example, it is now known that female preferences/attraction to male characteristics are affected by hormones in addition to, and beyond, cognition. Use of the birth control pill results in deferred child bearing and as a result may also affect a woman's selection of the father and his genetic characteristics. The de-feminization of the female population (also likely as a result of the use of the birth control pill) of the United States would be clear to see if people could directly compare

American women with women from traditional societies (or even from previous American generations), although this change was largely not thought to be a problem and possibly even desirable. It is unlikely that there were ever as many masculine women in the past as there are today, and it would be surprising if this did not contribute to the increase in lesbianism and reduction in family formation. Reduced femininity must also have decreased the attractiveness of women to men, just as emasculated men are less attractive to women.

Availability of birth control converts natural procreation into a volitional action choice that is much more difficult than a natural (or accidental) outcome (is there ever a right or perfect time to have children?). Birth control and the WRM merged with the powerful and mysteriously-promoted Zero Population Growth (ZPG) propaganda campaign of the 1960s and 1970s. As a result of these factors, procreation among the thinking or productive population has greatly declined or ceased in the face of new socio-cultural and career/financial consideration. It would be interesting to investigate who promoted these changes, what were their intentions and what is their current role in American life, but we can leave that investigation for others.

Among the less affluent in the United States, reduced procreation has not happened to the same extent. The same pattern is reflected around the world, even where there is a greater proportion and number of the less affluent. As a result, after decades of encouraging family size reduction in the United States and Europe the public is now told that more population is needed to sustain the costs of the economy and society. Actually this larger population is really needed retroactively from previous years when child bearing in the broad society was deferred in response to birth control propaganda! Instead of calling for an increase in native born child bearing like some governments have done, now opinion makers are calling for a new population in the United States to come from immigration of alien cultures and lower classes to sustain middle class America. If immigrants actually thought that their main job in the United States would be to support an ageing native-born middle class, would younger aliens come to the United States to work? How could this absurd situation ever have arisen?

There were other unnoticed or unconsidered affects from artificial birth control such as the loss of opportunity of women to use pregnancy as a method to enhance their social and economic status. This has had a huge but little noticed effect on society (linked to the increased and extreme class congregation noted in Coming Apart by Charles Murray) since it has now become possible to enjoy sex between classes without the possibility of offspring or formal relationship. This is an uncomfortable and complicated topic that cannot be fully addressed here, but several aspects can be noted. As observed in Coming Apart, region, culture and community (and my observed unintended consequences) have been greatly reduced as selection criteria for mating in favor of class (as newly defined), whereas they were formerly of great importance. That means that there is little non-performance and wealth-related criteria to help spread success in the gene pool, culture and region. This is an ominous development. In addition to the patterns pointed out in Coming Apart, other impacts are discussed below.

The recent historically high percentage of illegitimate children born to African-American women is well known. However, increasingly working class, lower middle class and poor white women are also single mothers and of mixed race children. This indicates that birth control has not been as effective in the lower classes as in the higher classes. In the higher classes much miscegenation is probably a result of Green Card fever or the desire of non-white men to "buy into" American society/culture. There is a slightly different trend of white men marrying non-white women, largely foreign, with the intention of having a more traditional family structure that is now hard to achieve in a endogamous white relationship.

It is now known that there can be health benefits to women from unprotected sex with men (this is not to encourage this in all situations), and also from pregnancy/child bearing. There are likely to be psychological benefits as well. These benefits are lost as a result of even the most basic artificial birth control. It may be that deferring childbearing and marriage for "self-realization" reasons may also result in increased health costs in later life.

Pornography

Birth control has changed the physical and social nature of sexual relations, and even social and physical behavior more broadly. Like filtered cigarettes requiring more effort to get the same stimulation from the same unfiltered cigarette, filtered sex appears to be having the same effect in encouraging more extreme and desperate efforts to get the same satisfaction. At the same time as sexual freedom has increased dramatically there has been a massive introduction of all sorts of pornography. We now know that the mind and body are very closely related. By removing so much of natural sexual relations from direct experience and placing them not in the individual's direct and personal imagination, but in a fabricated fantasy world, satisfaction with normal and natural sexual relations, not to speak of the near extinct courtship ritual, has certainly diminished. To the extent that abnormal desires and expectations are now created and met by pornography, the natural normal interpersonal sex drive must also have been reduced.

It was surprising how little objection has been raised to the presence of pornographic cinemas and shops, justified on the basis of freedom of speech. Allowing the presence of these businesses conveniently ignores the requirements for the industry which involve or encourage prostitution, abuse, etc. As with other rights movements, once pornography was firmly established in the culture on the basis of its supposed social benefits or rights of expression (reference the history of Hugh Hefner of <u>Playboy</u>), a campaign for all its negative aspects to also be accepted soon followed. All manner of behavior from prostitution to pedophilia is now on its way toward legitimization.

Environmental and Economic Factors

While on the subject of external forces affecting sexual relations and family structure we also must consider the impact of changes in behavior, environment, diet and cultural propaganda on human beings in the form of mental, physical and hormonal nature. Recent research has suggested that watching television reduces metabolism and results in weight gain, and that environmental pollution creates internal stress which subtly increases many physical illnesses. Hormones in the food chain are known and intended to bring major effects on animals and must also have a substantial impact on man. Some have even suggested that in rich countries the human form itself is changing due to fattening diets and reduced physical exertion (presented in its hypothetical conclusion in the movie <u>Wall-E</u>). The historical behavior patterns, thought processes and even biological nature of human beings are also likely to have changed as a result of such external factors. A good friend of mine once suggested that the use of atomic energy had disturbed some universal equilibrium and may have resulted in unknown human changes. Validating that would certainly require much more sophisticated analysis.

The separation of culture, community and reproduction from mating and family formation has contributed heavily to increased divorce, in the increasingly reduced cases where actual marriage takes place. This has created a further confusion of identity by creating multiple relationships of varying natures; and diffusing attention and priorities among various individuals and cultures. Not only this, but there is also additional cost of time and money to establish and maintain the increasing number of short-lived relationships. By entertaining these multiple relationships there is inevitably a lost focus on essential culture, since these are increasingly not guided by restricted family and core cultural groups.

By delaying family formation and reproduction there are naturally direct and indirect increased medical costs, as is evidenced by the increased physical problems of recent generations. Delay in childbearing results in complicated, expensive and unnatural conception procedures and in reduced family size. Moreover a new generational structure for reproduction is created where parents approach the historical ages of grandparents. This, too, will have a major impact on the relations between parents and children. Moreover, having none, one or two children also affects the family in dramatic ways. Having no children increases the present orientation of a couple and having only one or two children reduces the experience, knowledge and contact base which larger families can provide.

Delayed family formation also results in high costs for the independent living. Given these trends some have suggested that serial monogamy is the preferred relationship for the modern world, but this also incurs higher costs than those for traditional families. We also have to ask whether illegitimacy is bad in itself, or if it is just an extra challenge due to its lack of natural family support. Moreover, is illegitimacy any worse than broken homes or small/no child families. Since the need of the human race is to reproduce, and of different races to maintain their existence, what is the proper reproduction policy for a society with no common culture, but of a large population with increasingly separate cultures?

As hard as it is to believe, some years ago an optimistic voice was raised that Hispanics were family-oriented and therefore would be a positive contribution to American society. It remains to be seen if this is really true, even if we do not explore the meaning of whether a pro-family orientation is a virtue in and of itself. Within the

Hispanic community the pro-family orientation means a male dominated household. However, almost all people probably want to perpetuate their line and could be called pro-family. The only anti-family group might be radical extremists of various stripes. It is interesting that Hispanics were positively promoted as pro-family at the same time as parenting was generally a declining characteristic and not much encouraged in most of the core established American culture. As a result, a pro-family orientation might no longer even be an American virtue in and of itself since it is now in broad dispute. Moreover, the Hispanic community is now also facing a challenge to its family structure.

Child Farming - Adoption and Procreation Mating

Since the cultural adoption of birth control and delay/rejection of marriage, unusual, odd, and bizarre methods of family-building have become more common. Parenting is degenerating to the point where it is like keeping pets. Adoption by traditional married couples of children from other races and cultures has become more visible. What is the benefit of this? It assumes that nothing matters - not that the adopting parents don't want a child of their own culture, and not the heredity of the adopted child.

Since marriage is no longer needed for reproduction, single women and homosexuals have undertaken assisted birthing, volitional impregnation, and adoption to create families. With the move to legalize same sex marriage, acceptance of other previously rejected and illegal social structures such as polygamy, polyandry, near-relative marriage and underage marriage (arguably justified since our environment and diet now result in earlier puberty) will soon enter the public debate. This will provide a full range of confusing social structures which bear little resemblance to historical or traditional families. Is this a good strategy to sustain a society?

As if recent commercialization and privatization of culture had not destroyed enough authentic cultural experience, the loss of cultural memory as a result of miscegenation and lack of common culture, deferred family-building and population replacement by adoption and assisted conception will certainly wipe out most of what's left simply because it will be too difficult to find time, means or an appropriate culture to perpetuate.

Chapter 9. Alternative Sexual and Behavioral Rights

Overview

Following the revolutions of the CRM and the WRM which focused on the, at the time, largest potential conflicts in American society, the relativist philosophy began to extend to more controversial and uncharted areas. One of these was that of homosexuality.

Although it is traditionally considered to be outside of core social behavior and disapproved of in the Western World, in the Post-World War II period there has been increasing debate about the nature and origin of homosexuality. The main issue used to be whether it was natural or unnatural; willful or instinctive. The main question was whether there should be discrimination toward individuals because of their nature which they could not change. There had been such discrimination throughout history in order to preserve the species, but the perceived need to preserve one's own kind had nearly vanished in the Post-World War II period. As we have seen in the previous chapters, over the course of a short period of time in Europe and the United States, the idea had emerged that it was wrong to discriminate on any grounds (except on discrimination itself), since it was unfair to place disabilities on anyone, ultimately extending to criminals, the mentally ill and physically disabled. Of course this was absurd since it forces a counter discrimination against those who are by their nature and beliefs, primary order discriminators.

The issue of discrimination and counter-discrimination has been a poorly investigated point with respect to many economic theories of public good such as that of John Rawls. I suggest that discrimination is not an extraneous entity and obstacle to economic optimization, but is part of the nature and values of individuals and societies which are just as important as any transactional benefits that concern economists. Let us imagine a hypothetical scenario where there are two individuals where one of them either has resources that the other wants or resists a desired association with the other. Basically the two individuals are equal in some fundamental way, except that one wants to make claims on the other. If we support those claims we mean that the other party does not have a legitimate claim to withhold his resources or preferences. On what basis do we make such a decision? Ultimately, it means that there is no equality in life and that resources, preferences and decisions must be allocated either by individuals voluntarily with unequal outcomes, or by coercion from others (who would they be and by what right?) also with unequal outcomes. In one case an un-coerced outcome results and in the other a coerced outcome - both unequal.

American society was not historically concerned with the causes of homosexuality; only considering that it was a deviant behavior and not sanctioned by society. Unlike in Nazi Germany where homosexuals were reportedly persecuted, or in ancient Greece or Imperial Britain where homosexual relations may have had the nature of a ruling class fashion, in America homosexuals, as distinct from homosexuality, were largely left alone to live privately, but without the freedom for public demonstration. This is the origin of the now almost irrelevant phrase "coming out of the closet," since they could function in society only by hiding their behavior (although their nature was largely subconsciously known by society).

After the CRM and WRM, the next movement to emerge was the homosexual "rights" movement (HRM). Initially the argument made for this movement was to allow freedom of natural behavior, as if all natural behavior could be accepted. After the initial Trojan horse gambit the movement extended its claims further to justify homosexual behavior as a lifestyle choice free of natural behavior justification, although homosexual preference cannot be sustained under normal historical conditions or support the American social contract.

Homosexuality has always been present biologically and even socially, but due to its natural inability to reproduce the species (soon to be overcome) has not generally been sanctioned. In American society there have always been homosexuals in various aspects of life and their function has been as normal as their abnormal behavior would allow. Recently issues such as homosexual marriage, legal and property rights have been raised claiming the status of civil rights, or worse, human rights, whatever those are. The HRM has gone beyond the initial objective of removing any legal disabilities, if any, to the objective of establishing homosexuality as a valid lifestyle choice which must be accepted with the same status as other lifestyle choices. This arrogant challenge has even resulted in the adoption of children by homosexuals.

Since homosexuals are broadly covered by the relativist philosophy spawned by expanded civil rights interpretations, it has been increasingly difficult to restrict their freedom in general society. As a result, since they are disproportionately engaged in creative professions, their expanded audacity, behavioral activism and perversity are delivered to society in an attractive, powerful, pervasive and persuasive manner. In the end, expansion of freedom for homosexuals is anti-social and economically damaging to society. What fundamental benefit do they provide to society when they do not reproduce and present only a single generation view of society without providing preservation of the species? The homosexual single lifetime contribution of products such as enhanced interior design and dramatic arts is not enough to justify expansion of single-lifetime oriented values (although single lifetime orientation with no inter-generational exchange is also rapidly becoming the norm among heterosexuals).

The original claims of the CRM, WRM and HRM were that traditional social norms prevented them from exercising basic rights, but these claims rapidly spread to claims for the "right" of acceptance, although the withholding of that right was also a "right" of someone else. This acceptance is not the same as freedom from coercion, but is the surrender of a preference and forced confirmation by others at the very least. In this case the HRM is making a claim and those not part of the HRM are surrendering a right. We have seen in the CRM (Black, Afro-American, African-American) and WRM (Ms instead or Miss and Mrs.) that it is acceptable for aggrieved groups to expropriate a name for themselves that they consider complimentary, such as "gay" for homosexuals, and to force society to accept its new meaning in place of its historical meaning. Such expropriation cannot be valid since there is a zero sum gain of rights, preferences and associations, a reality that modern societies would be well advised to remember.

Using this rights claim pattern, ultimately every individual, to the extent that he deviates from any norm, may claim not only acceptance, but even further, entitlements. All rules are created on the basis of some norm, by either the powerful, majority or a common aspiration. If homosexuality may not face disability, what about bigamy? Some Mormons and Africans, and the Islamic Religion accept bigamy. What is the reason for making it illegal in the United States? Public health? Fairness? What about cousin marriage, polyandry, vaccinations, home schooling, religious holidays, other holidays, other work preferences. What is the difference between a belief that is protected, a cultural value that is protected, and just a preference or taste or tradition which is not? Is it possible for all beliefs and behaviors to be equally approved by and financially supported by society? Of course it is not possible, but once a dominant behavior and social structure, such as that of the traditional middle class, is no longer given preference, all other structures become equally valid in theory. Thus, the challenge to open-ended equality and democracy.

Chapter 10. Diversity Rights

Overview

The various rights movements considered in previous chapters initially developed along isolated tracks but through a domino effect. However, once they reached a combined critical mass, they collectively became a single large diversity rights umbrella movement (DRM) that can agglomerate almost any minority or dissident group. *This has created a large new American community that shares only the social contract of opposing traditional values, social structures and heritage, but sharing almost no other core objectives.*

In the latter decades of the 20th Century individual groups and government advocated various diversity rights which ultimately were accepted and accommodated by other groups, institutions and private business. By the second decade of the second millennium, however, claims for diversity are almost as regularly made by institutions themselves as they have become comfortable with and prosper from, the new diversity power and management structure and the market benefits it provides.

Diversity rights have come to represent an ideology which considers that there are benefits to having a limitless range of social or feature (the best way to describe some) groups. This is a major departure from previous American and most human society. Today in the United States, gone is the need to have common social and cultural standards that all should meet. Now having special (or hybrid) characteristics is a competitive advantage. Unifying social and cultural characteristics that once created institutions are now seen as liabilities. This has introduced a reverse discrimination whereby so many places are set aside for diversity that the majority community (if there is any longer such a thing) must naturally itself become a minority - but a uniquely disempowered one. Recent generations embrace the new diversity values they are taught in the absence of any other American social contract. The practical situation has reached the point where extensive diversity goals now are difficult to meet due to the absolute limit of even marginal candidates, necessitating recourse to greater international recruitment that provides global in addition to national diversity.

Diversity rights have quickly developed into the concept of multiculturalism over a very short span of time. Prior to the 1990s such a concept was largely unknown and irrelevant. People were what they were - and that usually was something. The various rights movements described in previous chapters broke down the shared characteristics of the American people and created a buffet environment where one could pick and choose any combination of artificial behaviors and characteristics for one's life and identity. This was further expanded by intercultural marriages or simply social breeding. So-called multiculturalism was possible because there was no longer an authentic community for most people in America, and all aspects of community could be directly and individually obtained from the consumer market. In this commercial market environment maximum social diversity would be a benefit in allowing the maximum number and type of products for expression of culture. Since all culture could in theory be broken down into innumerable pieces, no culture would be a misfit, only different combinations of pieces. But culture is not a market good, and all combinations of pieces do not make cultures.

American democracy no longer has any significant cultural context - only a shared value of diversity from any historical norm. However, diversity by definition is the lack of common culture and history, so the embrace of diversity has brought with it the loss of culture and history. Diversity as the new social structure combined with the drive for so-called equal rights and equal opportunity means constantly changing standards away from any norm and sometimes even from partial convergences. In place of previous respect for other cultures when restricted to their natural environments there is now the desire to establish additional alien cultures and behavior as part of and beneficial to American society, even though this has been presenting social problems for decades.

Such an unprecedented situation has never been experienced before in human history. Whereas previous multi-national empires and multi-ethnic states have existed, the lack of a dominant culture, and the fabrication of "custom" mixed cultures has not. Therefore we can infer that traditional political economy is not designed to support this structure and that it can only survive under the special conditions that support the United States today; namely a non-production economy established by the Dollar as the world reserve currency.

Since there is no common standard to be met for success in the "new" America, increasingly various forms of tribalism and nepotism have gained acceptance. How is this so? Of course there has always been positive discrimination in favor of powerful minorities. What was unique in the American experience was the significant and institutionalized rule of the middle class majority. It was this that was the great achievement of American democracy. Now that so-called formal negative discrimination against some weaker minority groups has largely been eliminated, there is now positive discrimination in institutions and business in favor of weak minorities in addition to the traditional minority power groups within the broader majority. The group that is lost in this transaction is the so-called majority, or more accurately, the fleeting plurality, since the dissection of society into many minorities means that there is no longer any practical holistic majority - only individuals that cannot be classified as a minority. The natural pathway to success is to emulate the culture of the dominant powers in society. Since there is not really a single dominant power in America, it is necessary for one to choose a single minority, or multiple minorities to associate with, or as that is increasingly not possible for some, to associate with one of the transcending professional guilds that in effect make up other privileged minorities. Multiculturalism has led to diversity rights, minority preference, internal social decay and rejection of any unifying features.

Language Rights

Along with a common national border and government, one of the greatest assets of the American people was English as a common language. Even though immigrants came to the United States with different languages, all but a few small groups found it practical to adopt English as their main or only language by the 1960s. The use of one language reduced many costs and restrictions in government and business and contributed to prosperity at home and abroad (from promoting English as the international language). Then sometime after the 1960s the idea of so-called bilingual education began to surface.

It is important to understand how this took place. Throughout American history there had been various organizations that sought to help immigrants to learn English as well as to provide their own special education in their traditional languages and customs at their own expense as a supplement to standard English education. Immigrants to America had wanted to learn English and were eager and grateful for the opportunity to learn it. Then suddenly there was an issue of bilingual education and information. In the early 1970s Sen. Hayakawa of California established a movement to make English the official language of the United States (there has never been an official language in the United States), but this movement was not able to achieve its objectives and faded away after the Senator's death.

The apparent reasons for the push for bilingual education were the increasing intrusion of government into education and all aspects of life; and the increase of immigration to the United States of people from the Southern Americas. Many of these people had a language other than Spanish as their first language. Others were of European stock with various cultures, and of course from the Cuban hegira many of whose members theoretically expected to return to Cuba. It could be seen, though, that the main target group was the indigenous and mestizo people whose only link with any modern culture was with the Spanish Language. Until that time there had been no significant problem to learn English from any other groups.

Bilingual services were not raised as a public policy issue, but rather implemented by government fiat. This was framed in terms of public convenience and efficiency initially, but soon became a rights claim. Although the initial focus was on Spanish, it soon expanded to bilingual services for all other languages as well. Over several decades immigration from Spanish speaking countries increased to the point where even those of advanced culture who would normally have acquired English as a first or second language, were encouraged to become a new privileged minority through linguistic and other social services.

Although the core issue had been that of separate supplemental linguistic services in Spanish, as with other rights claims described in earlier chapters, this claim too soon moved to the public domain as a "language" right to be given place alongside English. Since most immigrants know the value of English in the United States, this was not an action designed to support integration into American society, rather it was a limited benefit to a minority recreating the facility of its native place to be paid for by the general American society.

This initial bilingual education policy has expanded with great speed and energy to include a drive to include Spanish as a de facto second national language. It is interesting that the core interest in bilingual education has only been in Spanish, and that Spanish is the only language of sufficient use to be positioned to significantly disrupt the American social contract. Moreover, the benefits to the United States of any cultural link with the Hispanic Americas seem to be limited in comparison with those with the rest of the world where populations are excited about using the English Language. Moreover, the costs of providing bilingual education and support are high, while the value of Hispanic labor input to the American economy is low. Although in comparison to English and other languages Spanish has limited cultural and economic interest for the United States, there has been a continuous effort to promote the study of Spanish in the United States.

In recent years there has been a curious trend among the media elite to pronounce Spanish words, in the way a Spanish speaker would instead of the way the word is pronounced in American English. This is especially curious because this is not the same for words from other languages even closer to and with much more affinity to English such as French. If someone would pronounce Paris as" Pahrri" people would think it was affected and humorous, yet on National Public Radio many talking heads think nothing about saying "Lattinno" or "Chi-lay". Why would this be so? Why would my local radio station introduce a bi-lingual classical music program? Is it really to help uneducated Spanish speakers in the United States to better appreciate classical music?

As an aside, we also have to ask why, when India or Burma changes the historical names of cities or even the country, should we adopt these? Most countries use names of foreign lands that they have based on their own experience. Looking back, why did we ditch our historical names and terms for China in the 1970s? Psychologically, it is clear that the objective of linguistic rights is to de-link subjects and conversation from a shared American cultural viewpoint and establish them as independent and self-defining.

Manipulation of the Language Culture

As if the bilingual Spanish Language rights movement was not devastating enough for national communications, the entertainment, educational and entitlement service class also began to manipulate English well beyond the natural language evolution. Initially there had been politicization of language to support the CRM with respect to all words which had any relationship with race. This was gradually expanded to include words with reference to all claimants to special rights. Largely this meant the restriction on the use of words with historical or judgment meaning. Later this was expanded to include even simple observation words that could imply preference or judgment. A further stage came with the creation of new words and terms for objectives - and supposed disabilities of - claim holders.

This process continued with the flagrant distortion of the language in the most outrageous way by the use of homosexuals of the term gay as a positive judgment on themselves. Following this came all sorts of spin language for misfits and deviants. Normal people do not routinely need to invent such terms. Now we have reached the stage where only people who use language in a manner contrary to experience and with "political correctness," that is; in a distorted and misleading way, may participate in discourse outside of the most private life. The beginnings of total thought control through language control can even be seen in the big brother function of the Microsoft spell check and editing functions that make it difficult to use particular sentence structures and alternative spellings. And this, developed by a technical class not known for their great literary erudition!

I remember that even in the 2nd Grade one of my teachers was lecturing us kids not to use the word "nice". Through most of my education, teachers were criticizing us for the use of the subjunctive tense, and in recent years the United States Government has demanded reports using "action words." At the same time there has been a relaxation of the rules for the use of a singular verb for a plural noun or adjective, such as "there's," instead of "there are," by supposedly educated persons. Even there is also a development of speech patterns that differentiates women and some homosexuals. An example of this is "fry speech" where a statement has a question intonation at the end, implying the lack of confidence or judgment, or just a loose "devil may care" pronunciation of any word. This used to be associated with the Valley Girls mindless California female lifestyle, but has become fashionable with many women throughout the country. A good example of this was when one of my so-called colleagues in Afghanistan, with a Masters Degree from Harvard constantly talked about the need for "ssaells". Most people thought she meant "cells," but actually she meant "sales". Still, she could not bring herself to actually pronounce the word as "sayles". There are many other example of this juvenile fashion lingo that has entered mainstream use. The deep meaning of this is not simply sound, but attitude to the subject itself.

I will not even attempt here to explore the attempt, thus far only partially successful, to conduct war on our own culture and language by changing so-called gender and role references in language and behavior. Why should we complicate our lives by dropping the common third person singular pronoun "he" and replacing it with "he or she, him or her?"

Chapter 11. Education and the Arts

Education and the Skilled Workforce

One of the least discussed and debated government policies of the Post World War II period is that of education. As with the various rights movements already discussed, education rights also emerged from the peculiar Post-World War II economic wonderland of the United States. Education rights have not been clearly stated, but in practice they have grown to include universal access to education up to the graduate degree level. They also provide for the study of almost unlimited subjects, not coincidentally with an emphasis on promoting government social policies. This has resulted in a massive expansion of the university system with many colleges becoming universities and with universities expanding their departments and programs with virtually no limit or standards. As a result, much educational expenditure has been wasted on poor teaching, social policy, useless subjects and unqualified students.

At the same time, universities have developed themselves as business profit centers, through the use of laboratories, research centers; conference, sport and art performance; individual research and consulting, education-related services and a plethora of lesser activities. This has had a major effect on the economy because it has encroached on the traditional domain of the private sector with the benefit of extensive subsidies given to universities, especially public ones.

Establishment costs of professors and their apprentice graduate students are already covered by salaries and tuition, so that consulting and research activities are subsidized by fixed facilities and labor. When universities compete with the private sector the advantage of this subsidy as well as the un-costed background preparation time and opportunity to switch between institutional and business work can be dramatic. The extent of this operation has been increasing year by year as universities face new financial challenges. Moreover, because government subsidies require universities to support government social policies, universities have brought these policies into technical work to a greater extent than has the private sector. In addition, public universities can also use the power of eminent domain to acquire property, gain property tax exemption, and co-opt the political system by promoting student voter registration at temporary locations.

The establishment of universities as government supported and protected institutions is well on its way toward creating another branch of government whose existence and expansion are virtually guaranteed. After reaching a growth ceiling in the student affordability pool in the 1970s, a major expansion in government funding through grants and subsidized loans was implemented which increased university enrolment, but also which changed the finance of universities. Now, universities could become direct actors in obtaining funding for students that would be passed on to the universities themselves. As a result, universities became agents to find their own funding (students) rather than to select student buyers with funds or to fund students that had been selected. In the 1980s the pool of American students desiring admission to graduate school began to decline and places/public subsidies then began to be offered to foreign students. After the Year 2000 this subsidy to foreign students began to be extended to undergraduate programs as well.

Many American students were attracted to many of the new and pseudo-scientific disciplines which had no practical employment potential other than in the universities themselves, in institutions or in government. Other more practical Americans took up public contact jobs such as advertising, sales, promotion which required less university education, while the most privileged went into the guild-restricted professions of law, business and medicine that required more years of study. In addition to being attracted to admission to any university as a path to getting a visa, more talented foreign students less distracted by the temptations and social life of America, went into the technical fields and graduate study largely ignored by native-born Americans.

Once they also could get their Green Card or citizenship, foreign students often left their technical fields to be the boss or make more money in management or business, as would their children. As a result, contrary to what most Americans believe, these immigrants do not constitute a long term solution to the so-called need for skilled labor. Similarly, immigrant doctors working in small rural communities are not likely to remain there any longer than necessary and will most likely leave much more quickly than Jewish dry goods storekeepers did in previous generations. Immigrants with non-qualifying credentials in fields such as medicine could convert their qualifications through specialized schools such as medical schools in the Caribbean and then enter the United States work force through a path not really practical for Americans.

After obtaining education and residency at greatly subsidized rates with the connivance of universities and the government, many clever immigrants discovered that government social policies provided more opportunities to immigrants that are not available to most native-born Americans such as minority contract set-asides and small business administration loans. This is part of the explanation for immigrant control of small hotels and convenience stores throughout the country, as well as ownership of government and international contracting firms. Some foreign students, such as Chinese, returned home to introduce American knowledge at home for more effective competition with Americans, or stayed in the United States to work in sensitive jobs that would allow them to spy on American operations in this country. Others, such as Indians, set up businesses in the United States to be used to sponsor immigration of fellow nationals for work at lower wages and with less security than native Americans would obtain. Really clever immigrants would set up businesses in the United States and then link them with off-shore employment in their homelands.

With the above conditions in mind we should ask why subsidized education combined with broad free trade have been introduced by government fiat. Although this subject is rarely discussed, when there is some discussion, the justification given is that this policy improves American competition and the quality of the work force. However, it is clear that the result of the United States education policy is to restructure the distribution of the workforce (activities as well as composition), economic power and social management in the country.

The Arts - "there's a riot going on"

Closely related to the rise of educational institutions as agents of the government and social revolution, is the introduction of entertainment masquerading as the so-called " the arts" which is probably the most surreptitious and insidious deception that has ever been perpetrated on the American people. For most of American history exposure to the so-called "the arts" was limited to a tiny part of the population, and was produced mainly by an even tinier misfit part of that group. For the most part "the arts" was literature of misfits attempting to document or explore their condition in society, unlike classical literature which explored the human condition and the meaning of life. Although this misfit literature was touted by arts mavens to be of importance and value, there is no broadly objective or historical justification for that position. Nevertheless modern misfit literature has continually been promoted and continued to degenerate.

In the 1960s and 1970s this misfit modern literature quickly replaced classical literature as the focus of study in schools and universities. Instead of using literature to introduce and reinforce time tested experience, values and judgment, new literature only introduced limited temporal and fringe, experience and issues. Since this was inserted as a replacement for and not a supplement to classical literature, it created the impression that the misfit world was somehow the real world. In this way the arts have become not really a separate subject, but actually an aspect or vehicle of education which seeks to change and distort the perception of reality.

There have always been opportunities for raucous and immoral entertainment suited to all classes, but this was infrequent and diversionary for most of human history, and did not interfere with the routine social structure as the core guide for the society. In the 20th Century urban areas created the critical mass, access and wealth to expand this perverse entertainment, which quickly generated the revenues, visibility and influence to make a claim to be part of "the arts." Local and immigrant misfits flocked to all aspects of the entertainment industry. This was further enhanced by immigrant misfits who were often better educated and more clever than the locals.

This set the stage for the continuous presence of debauched entertainment to be promoted by new technologies in the urban centers. In addition, technologies became interwoven with expression and themselves became protected as freedom of speech in a totally new context. Anything and everything could be dreamed up and presented to appear as reality, rather than as just a personal idea on a known subject; even as a fantasy with no relationship to any known reality. Unlike open debate in the square of public opinion, the new entertainment now would be a continuous promotion of misfit ideas, yet it would be all one-sided without debating counterpoints, since the concept of "art" is subjective. As a result art promotes ideas, politics and social policy as propaganda with no counter-balancing facility to protect the consumers from idea fraud.

The Bolsheviks understood this benefit well and used it to control the Soviet Union for almost 80 years.

As with misfit literature, other aspects of entertainment developed to present pernicious and distorted experience and ideas. In the late 19th Century there were burlesque shows later transitioning into vaudeville, follies and ultimately radio, movies and television. Technology initially expanded the population and area coverage range for these, and later reduced the cost making more frequent access possible. Today the Internet makes the range and frequency of presentation almost universal and continuous. In addition, technology has made it possible to move from simple representation and "artistic" rendering to creation of complete alternative realities which appear to be representations of a reality that could be experienced by the viewer, but are often only misfit fantasies and dreams. Since much more time is spent in viewing this "alternative" reality than in experiencing "actual" reality, viewers begin to consider the alternative reality as the actual reality because that is all they have ever seen or experienced.

The intrusion of this one-sided political and social propaganda is found not only in numerous private businesses through their ubiquitous television monitors, but even in public spaces and government facilities. It was the drug- and anti-establishment-inspired arts that lobbied for and received government (mainly Federal) funding for mandated arts in public spaces. This was usually modern or avant-garde art that contrasted with the more staid and traditional buildings and open space in order to create a perceptual distinction as well as to provide patronage to so-called artists, chosen not by public acclaim, but by artist "peers". This was another way of promoting alternative reality, and conflict between traditional and so-called popular culture, and at the same time avoiding any debate between the two.

Chapter 12. Use of the Media to Restructure Cultural Reality

Overview

At the end of the tumultuous 1960s I attended a private conservative Christian school to escape manifestations of American social breakdown. There, my efforts at growing my hair long (or at least a little fuller), use of modern Bible translations and class projects (like designing a future city where there were no graveyards) brought me under suspicion of being "on the wrong track" and eventually forced me to leave. My nemesis, a graduate of the conservative Bob Jones University (which has since apparently recanted many of its original views for unknown reasons) and my science teacher, lived in a frill-free trailer just off the school entrance road with his family, and refused to have a television. I thought that was totally bizarre at the time, although now I can imagine how our society might have developed better if we had not had televisions, since we would not have been brainwashed with concocted and unrealistic images of reality, but instead would have viewed our own realities and invented our own dreams.

Through television and movies we imbibed a huge cultural presentation. Some of that presentation was broadly representative of our lives and/or a source of entertainment. Other was clear fantasy or pure myth. In the early days of television many programs depicted a reality that was broadly similar to what we had experienced or could observe such as the Honeymooners and Leave it to Beaver. We could imagine that some situations were like our own or other people's lives. Of course video entertainment naturally distorts reality by presenting only superficial situations and promoting desired objectives, but its mixed visual images have come to be associated with behaviors and values that are otherwise totally unrelated. Over time the programs began to present generally familiar settings, but with unfamiliar characters and situations, making it seem possibly real, such as <u>All in the Family</u> and <u>Happy Days</u>.

This style expanded over time into fantasy and myth programs that presented even less familiar settings that were only conceivable or imaginable such as the <u>Twilight Zone</u> and <u>Dallas</u>. Even science fiction programs were not truly alien, but situational variations from normal experience with conceivable themes, such as <u>Star Trek</u> and <u>Lost in Space</u>. Early program themes were about problems that were often created by the unknown and the alien in order to show the strength of the known, although later themes depicted challenges from outsiders or the new in order to show ourselves, our experience and our traditional values as being wrong. This can be seen in such seemingly innocuous programs as <u>Daniel Boone</u> and <u>Happy Days</u>. A precursor or response to the generation gap conflict of the 1960s was the broad use of children and youth to teach lessons to the parents in both television and movies on the pretext that new conditions the parents did not understand required change. By the late 1960s there was a plethora of television and movie attention to all forms of rebellion against the American mainstream and traditional values. Integrated with the anti-war and counterculture movements this regular propaganda was unexpected, challenging and ultimately terribly destructive to America.

Over time, the abnormal, fantasy environment of the entertainment industry attracted and created a so-called creative population that deviated from the mainstream society with the result that movies and television programming also began to diverge from mainstream social representations to representations of fringe groups and people such as <u>Three's Company</u>, the <u>Partridge Family</u>, etc. When they saw Woody Allen movies, most Americans had no reference from which to assess whether they were accurate portrayals of an unknown New York City culture, a generic metropolitan non-culture or just the experience of the isolated misfit, Allen. Throughout a good part of the 1970s the mix of television and movie presentations was fairly balanced between small town, country, big city and other typical environments, although African-Americans were mostly left out except for some token gestures. However, by the end of the 1970s a major change was taking place that would reverse that balance and focus more on metropolitan non-culture.

All of a sudden the portrayal of American life on television and in movies changed dramatically. It seemed as if historical and current America was a mainly metropolitan, liberal, non-traditional and service sector society, with traditional values and culture ignored or belittled.

Starting in the late 1960s Americans were suddenly deluged directly by urban, political and social media presentations, and shown that they had been sadly ignorant of many subjects that were of universal importance, although totally unrelated to their own experience and culture. This was a real epiphany in that the vast majority of Americans learned for the first time that there was an alternative environment and explanation for the society that they thought was theirs and that they knew.

Starting even earlier, perhaps even in the 1950s, cameo or bit player characters in films and television began to use Northeastern and urban, styles and language when portraying environments and cultures where that would not be expected. This was tolerated in the name of entertainment, but over time it added up to create the impression that these exceptional characters were normal in almost all environments and times.

Even more surprising was the replacement of the Lone Ranger and John Wayne self-reliant frontier heroes with the outsider crusader who waged battles against wrongs that had little meaning for most Americans, or that were even against the traditional culture. Even in television and movies there were frequently lawyers, journalists or investigators who subtly presented examples of the righteous outsider against the mainstream culture. In such cases the mainstream culture would be oppressing some outlying opinion or individual and the hero would enter the scene to save the day. In movies we often see an evil white man, an innocent African-American or other minority victim, and a crusading outsider. The motive behind the outsider's involvement is presented to be only the objective love of justice, and at the same time, a desire to fight traditional ideas and values.

These stereotypes are wrong and seriously misleading. Often a white male character might be a good family man and neighbor, or even a desperate worker trying to protect his job, yet is presented as a racist (whatever that means), supposedly full of hatred and destined to burn in a secular hell. At the same time, in comparison, oppressed African-Americans (and other minorities) were presented as decent, respectable people. It should always be remembered that oppression is always for a purpose and is not prima facie wrong. What is normally wrong is oppression of good or righteousness, but some oppression (of some people) is socially sanctioned in the form of laws, rules, asylums and prisons. Finally, the image of the crusading outsider implies that it is his nature that makes him a crusader for justice, but does not explain that he is an outsider in many ways and may not even have a relationship with the larger community. Being an outsider is not necessarily objective, since most social/cultural conflict resolution should take place *within* the community and not be imposed on it.

Examples of outsider crusaders can be found where the hero or heroine is more often than not of less than exemplary character, a misfit or an otherwise troubled individual such as in the movie "Erin Brockovich." In addition, often if not always, the oppressed individual would not be objectively good or exemplary; but justified by being oppressed. Over time this created the impression that all oppressed, suppressed or rejected misfits were somehow themselves otherwise examples to be admired and copied. Always the theme was the same in that the mainstream society was oppressive and wrong in exercising its value judgments on the unfortunate minorities and misfits and needed to be taught a lesson by the same. Ultimately it meant that either mainstream society was oppressing, taught a lesson or defeated, and that righteousness was on the side of the oppressed and their champions.

Weak attempts to control and restrict such propaganda were not successful because they objected to the subjects of video media, rather than to their misrepresentation and use as propaganda. Freedom of speech had already been captured as freedom of propaganda against traditional values.

Decline and End of Shared Experience

When Americans had a culture and lived in communities they shared many experiences and values. Even with the breakdown of real experiential communities we at least had a sort of community through free airwave radio and television. However, the 1970s saw the disappearance of the Honeymooners and the emergence of Three's Company. All of a sudden TV characters no longer represented familiar characters that were working at productive jobs, but independently rich, unemployed, working casual jobs, and always consuming. We didn't think anything of it then, but some people did notice the loss of many traditional patterns and activities in television programs. After the decline of physical communities, television became our virtual community of shared faux experiences. The introduction of cable TV with its innumerable segmented market niches for the promotion of business interests finally shattered even the veneer of an American community other than that of consumers in market niches which could never provide a national social cohesion.

Chapter 13. Misfit and Technical Elite Empowerment

Overview

The fundamental argument for the women's movement and the family revolution was the overriding imperative of independent self-expression. Yet, where in history is self-expression found as a basis for society? The power of the self-expression movement came largely from the extraordinary sense of self-importance held by the Post-World War II generation. This broad generational sense of self-importance was a form of national hubris which was in sharp contrast to the experience of historical societies. After all, most people do not have the capacity to need freedom of self-expression independent of existing social behavior norms? All societies provide freedom for self-expression which is usually sufficient for most people since they must function within that society. For those few individuals needing or desiring more freedom, ability to function within the social structure is tenuous and they are often expelled, exiled or ostracized.

Societies generally provide structures and patterns for individuals that enable them to function efficiently so that they don't have to recreate most knowledge, behavior and judgment, although some may see this as restricted freedom. Western societies since the Enlightenment have increasingly emphasized individualism, but for most of the period this has been a limited individualism built on the edifice of established society. However, in the United States, individualism now claims almost all of the social space, creating great inefficiencies and risking social anarchy. This is a more serious threat to the society because even persons with limited capacity for individual expression are encouraged to develop that capacity which they may not naturally have and in some cases would be a borrowed individualism. Not only does this create stress and expose confusion in individuals, but it also undermines the foundations of society, by removing the primacy and legitimacy of social guidance and support.

Traditional American society is a framework culture of a complete society that assumes minority groups will fit within the society "and only deviate to a limited extent". The currently emerging American "myth" in hubristic contrast assumes that American society can safely allow "full freedom of expression" to alien cultures, interests and investments, and those alien cultures, interests and investments will somehow limit themselves voluntarily to a harmless space within American society where there would be no risk of distorting or destroying common and traditional American institutions and thinking. This fallacy has been promoted by globalist intellectuals and misfits concentrated in cities along with the various rights movements as a type of "unity of disunity".

The preceding chapters have shown that the race, sexuality, gender and other rights movements have now become internal aspects of American society based on the assumption of "unity of disunity" and limited deviation. Manipulated in the right way, these movements involve sufficient population numbers to easily split the national society into unmanageable sub-groups. This is made even more inevitable with the broader self-expression movement that further breaks up each of these increasingly conflicting rights groups. The CRM, sexual, gender and self-expression movements essentially destroyed the structures of moral (having the status of accepted authority) social and cultural leadership. With the loss of this leadership there has also been the loss of the corresponding "followship." With the loss of leadership and followship, and hence unity, there was only one way that society could be managed - through manipulation and force of raw power.

This raw power for manipulation is different from the legitimate power that comes from society and culture. It is a statist power with the sole purpose of control and aggrandizement. It is difficult to institute statist power directly because of the resistance of at least some of the people whose freedom, status and assets may be threatened. Using classical warfare strategy the best approach is to avoid direct attack and use subterfuge. In the case of the most modern democratic states this has often been done by increasing distance between issues, deliberation and decisions, otherwise known as reduced transparency. Ironically, this has often been achieved in recent times under the guise of empowerment. This false empowerment essentially diverts the attention of the public to issues and procedures that have no meaningful impact on core decisions. Examples are the establishment of small government units for citizen participation despite the fact that fundamental decisions are only made at higher levels, and where extensive public consultation procedures are implemented only for the purpose of reporting and process rather than as actual decision making inputs.

As long as basic government and management issues were practical and understandable to the common man it was possible to organize political issues so that debate and battle could be focused and accessible. Actually there were few perennial political issues other than taxes and economic rights (although from time to time new major issues such as slavery, suffrage, war, etc. came up, but these were also mostly, on their face, simple and straightforward). The limitation on political issues was due to the limited size of and expectations from government. There were many other issues, but those by and large did not enter into the political sphere, remaining within the family, community and larger cultural group. Starting with the FDR New Deal programs, government began to take responsibility for most aspects of individual lives. This was due to the presumption by the ruling elites (or wannabe ruling elites) that individuals could not manage their own affairs because of broader forces beyond their control. Of course there is some truth to this in the face of long term growth of cultural mixing, population sizes and urban concentration. As a result, the challenges resulting from the

Great Depression (an economic crisis) were used as an opportunity to expand government into aspects of life which had otherwise been independent of the American (or other) political economy.

Over several decades the "emergency" activities of the New Deal created bureaucracies and management structures which operated at higher strategic levels beyond the local community and required specialized experience and training. This brought new demands on colleges and universities to specialize in management and management-related areas rather than traditional and classical liberal arts. All subjects eventually became analytical, technical and managerial rather than routine and transparent. This is well explained by Immanuel Wallerstein in his writings on world systems analysis. The result was broad and extensive. The influence of traditional values, history and culture was excised in favor of a pseudo-scientific technical structure for most subjects. Not only did this remove the possibility to understand even common subjects from the average man, but it also created a community and culture-free class of educated "technocrats" who could migrate like carpetbaggers to almost any place and work without any need to have any relationship with or values in common with the community. The range of work requiring such "technocrats" has expanded massively to the point where almost all "professional" jobs are filed by such persons. As a result of affirmative action and anti-discrimination rules, "professionalized" jobs now require national profile representation that often actually requires the jobs to be filled by individuals alien to the community who were often already similarly selected through the educational process.

As a result of this technocratization of work, city planners, lawyers, educators, social workers, medical practitioners, even engineers (trained in sub-disciplines such as so-called value engineering, etc.) could be from anywhere, even outside the United States, as long as they had the sanction of their guild or met diversity goals. It became almost impossible for the common man to question or oppose them, since they were comfortably paid and sanctioned to advance their professional work while the common man taxpayer was busy at work and home. Since the common man could generally not have access to the privileged and often arcane professional tools and assumptions he would have to question decisions only on the basis of his non-scientific subjective preferences. As a result, technocrats have become culturally and operationally separated from the regulated public. This chasm became even more pronounced when government and private management also integrated affirmative action and other unrelated agenda in their management decisions. Beyond this, decisions such as long term investment in energy and future planning have moved away from a focus on current residents (constituents) to unknown and hypothetical future beneficiaries (clients) who must be represented against the current residents and whose interests are defended by the technocrats.

The result was not only an intrusion of government into provision of services (hardly present for most of the country's history), but ultimately also into regulation of all aspects of life. This was not just a cultural regulation such as requiring a certain number of years of schooling and teaching of certain subjects (with government chosen textbooks), but also practical regulation of implementation procedures and techniques. The best example of this practical regulation is that of zoning. One of the basic freedoms and rights of Americans is property ownership. However, ownership means freedom to use property as one wishes and for one's personal gain. However, government in most places has long since usurped this power through zoning and management by, most often, non-local technocrats. Before one starts to imagine that property rights can only be infringed by a socialist conspiracy, it should be noted that the actual result of technocratic capitalism is the concentration of property rights in the hands of a limited number of developers/property managers who can work the regulatory system and meet government and professional standards. Hiring the architect, zoning lawyer, planner, engineer, etc. that are required for most successful zoning applications is too expensive, complicated or risky for the common man. As a result, a higher scale of business organization and operation is needed to collaborate with the government technocrats, who have in essence become private sector development partners who limit competition to bigger and favored players.

This process can be observed in all areas of the economy and aspects of society. Government, insurance, banking and professional regulation of medical charges, licenses and business operations may at first sound reasonable and beneficial. However, the real purpose and result of this regulation is control - not only by the operators of business, but by unaffected salaried (and sometimes commissioned) technocrats. This overregulation has come to mean that an individual must use a "guild" judgment and not his "personal" judgment. As a result, "personal" word or "subjective" assurance cannot be honored within the technocratic system. The direct and visible individual is no longer the holder of power, rather it is the invisible guild. As a result, the trust authority and legitimacy basis for transactions and methods - the essence of Common Law - no longer exists and has been replaced by simple, hidden, supposedly objective, but often disguised power.

In the same way that Wallenstein observed in false technocraticization of the social sciences, job standards have also been increasingly guildized to create a false standard of professional and performance quality. This has ultimately led to a warped use of rules and law instead of practical objectives and logic. Moreover, valid discussion and conflict have been suppressed and replaced by impersonal assignment of gains and losses - the so-called cost-benefit and alternatives analysis in which the advocated position almost always wins because the rules and analysis are controlled by the advocates.

It is not liberal or conservative, government or big business, or ownership, but technical, regulatory and management control that is the prime feature of this technocratic guild environment. Daniel Bell observed in his The Coming of Post-Industrial Society, that the Soviet Union and the United States increasingly shared more and more features of regulation and control that brought into question the practical meaning of their professed ideological differences. In the Soviet Union industry was government managed and regulated, while in the United States it is mostly privately managed, but government regulated (and in India large industry was government planned and regulated, but implemented by private oligopoly business).

The key point here is that technocrats (read: outsiders and misfits) found skills and an environment to empower themselves over traditional social and political structures. This has been done from the smallest town to the largest agencies in the federal government. In Coming Apart, and in Bobos in Paradise of David Brooks, some examples of the types of jobs and individuals who have claimed these opportunities are given. However, both books focused more on the top elite rather than the broader job structure. If we look more carefully at that broader structure we find that the staffing of county or town planner positions follows the same pattern at a lower level as that of Goldman Sachs alumni who float between the Department of the Treasury, boards of major universities and corporate management. That pattern is the aggregation and transfer of power and rights away from the experience of the core society and common man to a super-experiential control of ideas and the decision making process by technocrats. As this system developed the energy needed to create and empower the technocrats was achieved while the energy needed to remain a technocrat has been reduced.

As touched on in <u>Coming Apart</u> by Charles Murray the higher level technocrats have developed their own culture and survival strategy, but largely do not promote this as a valid example for non-technocrats. In <u>Coming Apart</u>, Murray chooses to limit his assessment of this behavior to socio-economic indicators. It is not just their personal and family behavior that technocrats generally do not promote and evangelize (in contrast to their political ideas, such as those discussed in the previous sections, which they actively promote), but their ethnic, regional and traditional cultural identities. The much deeper significance of this is that the technocrats at all levels have pulled away from their origins and communities so that they no longer have a local rather than professional or class identity. This can be seen from their marriages, religion (or lack of it), adopted children, residential segregation, and general distance from the communities from who they sprang.

The consequences of this structural change in social terms are huge, but so too are the economic and political impacts. The change greatly reduces local community linkages for upward mobility, aspiration, morally uplifting guidance, and the flexibility that creates opportunities for individual genius and initiative. Thus, the conditions that made America's great development possible before the 1970s are no longer present. Gradually increased social benefits had given away the American labor cost advantage. Then international education and aid gave away American technical advantages. Technocratization of management removed the power of the common man from design. Finally only the power of the United States Dollar as the international reserve currency was left, but as the world changed and become much more competitive that too is declining. Other than the consumption and social welfare benefits derived from the United States Dollar as the international reserve currency, technocratization may be the only structural cultural and historical product of Post-World War II America.

In his classic book, <u>The Leisure Society</u>, Thorsten Veblen spoke about the masses imitating the elite and is remembered for his idea that shielding ones skin from the sun was fashionable since it indicated freedom from manual labor until the elite discovered tennis and stylish suntans. It is too bad that that Veblen is not here today to update his ideas on status behavior. Certainly things have changed drastically since the 1960s. Prior to the CRM American society enforced some degree of behavioral and value conformity and aspiration with deference to the power of the middle class majority. That deference was essentially a type of civility.

As a result of the statist technocratic structure which has taken over in the latter part of the 20th Century with its socially and culturally alien and sometimes adversarial technocracy, social misfits and radicals not bound to communities and tradition have become better qualified as technocrats, wise men and respected elders. As a result there has been a dramatic increase in the number of homosexuals, women, recent immigrants and other minorities in the technocratic/elite structure. The odds of this revolution occurring naturally are very low. The odd lyrics and slogans of the radicals and outsiders are now taken as reality and scripture while the Bible is distorted and defamed. The aggressive, disruptive and disrespectful have become the leaders and role models. Ultimately it is only those technocrats who have no traditional or community cultural values that are taken into the power structure, but what then is the basis for their judgment and truth? The ultimate answer is - their guild knowledge.

Conservatives often blame the reduction of personal liberty on "liberals," but it is more accurate to point the finger at the socio-cultural "misfits" who have become technocrats. This class often dislikes or hates traditional and mainstream society, and wants to destroy it or at least to render it powerless to impose its values. These technocrats can be either Democrats or Republicans, and may be conservative or liberal on different issues. Illegal, fraudulent or ill-advised immigration has further diluted the national identity, consensus and social contract making it easier for clever misfits to be successful despite their conflict with local communities by further ensuring that there are no shared standards in behavior, education, history, language, and family values. This has created an environment where technocrats in all sectors can "break free" from the masses. The last bastion of freedom from technocratic rule is the domain of state's rights which supports local self-rule, but both Federal Government and United Nations supporters are continuously working to destroy this structure and freedom.

Most technocrats and technocratic organizations no longer truly "fit in" with any traditional group. Instead they use and manipulate the various groups for their interests. An interesting example of this at the political level is the election of Barack Obama as President of the United States. Obama had no significant local political support base and used various unrelated "vote banks" such as the heretofore unknown "swing" racially/culturally non-identifying group to win the Presidency. Indian politics has long relied on piecing together numerous unrelated "vote banks" for its elections and American politics has now adopted the same approach, although America's vote banks are entitlement lobby groups rather than ethic and cultural groups as in India.

The election of Barack Obama marks a high point where American society removed itself from de Toqueville's local government reality to live in a fantasy world of systems and procedures. The United States Dollar as the international reserve currency, technology and technocracy with a highly developed system of rules and decision making techniques have alienated decisions and consequences from the mass public. The absence of any means for the common man to enter public policy discourse, or influence social and community standards due to the structure of technocratic rule is itself a type of violence for social control. It is not surprising that the final tool left to the common man for redress - physical violence (starting from corporal punishment of children to ownership of firearms to physical intimidation) - is greatly opposed by the technocrats and elites because they seek to control without the effort or opposition that physical violence could introduce. The statist system with its regulation and obfuscating standards claims to reduce social risks, but it does so by reducing opportunity and freedom.

Chapter 14. Sex, Drugs and Rock and Roll

The Generation Gap

Closely related to the establishment of the statist technocratic system and empowerment of a social misfit and radical class of technocrats is the emergence and power of the Baby Boom Generation in the United States. The Baby Boom Generation was closely identified with the Vietnam War, but it was the generation's demand for freedom and leisure to enjoy sex, drugs and rock and roll that defined it.

Probably there has always been an eagerness of youth to assume the roles of adults, but historically it has been necessary to first gain the core cultural knowledge which elders have. This necessarily put some obstacles and delays in the way of previous younger generations assuming power. However, with the rapid changes in society and technology, and with increased leisure and affluence, youth in the Post-World War II period began to imagine that they had an independent claim on an early transition to social - and ultimately political - power. In is ironic that this claim was made against the authority of those that Tom Brokaw has called (probably with poor insight) the "greatest generation."

In fact many of the early leaders of rock and roll, and rock music were born prior to the end of World War II, yet it was largely the Post-World War II Baby Boomer generation that carried that vanguard's initiative to assert its claim to revolution against the "system." Because of the music, drugs and social revolution, there truly became a generation gap, which was exploited as a weakness in the previous generation, rather than as a strength of the baby boomers. As a result, the baby boomers did not have to learn the cultural information and behavior of previous generations, but by sheer force introduced their new experience which was ultimately embraced by their own parents - child is father to the man.

The Vietnam Experience

During the 1960s and 1970s most people thought they understood the Vietnam conflict as a struggle for control of that Vietnam between communist and anti-communist forces. People either liked or supported one side or the other with an accepted underlying reality as a common point of reference. Some said that it was a necessary war against communist influence and expansion, some said war for any purpose was wrong, some suggested it was right for the Vietnamese to oppose external powers, and others that it wasn't any of our business. Some said that the situation was presented with lies, but that mainly referred to the methods used to present and justify responsive actions (like sending American advisors rather than soldiers) rather than about questioning the essential reality of the struggle between communist and anti-communist forces. No one really suggested that American involvement was primarily a method to test military weapons, to gain international influence, to provide employment to massive numbers of less educated Americans, or to achieve other domestic political objectives.

Was there any truth to any of the debating positions of the 1960s? Yes, there was probably some truth to all of them. What was the result of the whole mess? Finally - lot of spending, death, domestic strife, social change - and Indochinese immigrants to the United States. We fought communist (Chinese, Russian?) influence and supported the royalists and French colonial collaborators. In the end we resettled large numbers of those, including ethnic Chinese, to the United States and other countries when we lost the war. Where were the anti-war protesters then? Where were the protests against the reeducation and retributions which followed the fall of our puppet government there? Were there any street protests against the excesses that followed in Cambodia? Going further, where were the protests against the Chinese Cultural Revolution?

So ultimately was there any sincerity to the protests about the war in Vietnam, or about the conditions in most other countries? Probably little. Maybe it was only that the spoiled children of the elite just wanted to enjoy their un-earned privilege and party it up (maybe the same situation was behind the Tian An Men Square demonstrations). True issues such as the absurdity of part time and limited warfare really were not really on the table then or afterwards, and in fact became part of standard American military procedure. Neither was the right of a people to national self-determination. In fact the only things that mattered was loss of life, national wealth, national disillusionment and the effect the war had on the spoiled baby boomers themselves. Matters of principle and actual policy issues did not seem to have any meaning.

Since the spoiled baby boomers - under conditions of the unnatural Post-World War II national prosperity and as a powerful demographic bubble - managed to get out of that mess on their own terms they just kept on moving without looking back or being responsible to anyone but themselves as the big winners in the lottery of history. Having emerged victorious from the 1960s, with no significant cost to themselves, the baby boomers continue to expect to have things their way with no cost to themselves and to insist on freedom to self-righteously do as they like – and to dismiss the values that matter to others.

Baby Boomer Privilege

For those of us that grew up with a vanishing historical American culture and the establishment of individual leisure activities unconstrained by morality and community, it seems that sex, drugs, and rock and roll have always been available and in the same form as we ourselves have experienced. The sexual revolution was treated in more detail in an earlier section. Historically we can see that some form of drug use has been a feature of most human societies. However, drug use (as broadly defined to include alcohol) has been mainly among those who could afford the purchase or harvesting cost, and among those who could afford the use (capacity and time) cost. Very few societies could afford drug use by large numbers of its members or for large periods of time (longer than festivals) simply because of the cost, and loss of time and ability.

In the United States after World War II the affluence created by the Breton Woods world financial system allowed so much excess wealth and productive capacity that a whole generation was free for leisure until their 30s or later, with no responsibilities, moral obligations or fear of starvation. Some of this leisure was devoted to recreational drug use, but to meet the huge demand to fill time, the music industry emerged in earnest with rock and roll.

Before rock and roll most lyrics were simple and expressed common experience and feelings. Since these were common most everyone could play the tune on an instrument or sing, so there was limited scope for commercialization. Since these were shared experiences there was little unique art in the music and listeners were rarely shocked although they were generally entertained and amused.

While there was nascent music production earlier in the 20th Century mainly with big band and swing music, it was in the 1950s when the music industry really began to develop. It appears to have had two main streams that converged and diverged throughout the 20th Century: folk and rock/pop. Folk music had long had a rich tradition in the United States, particularly in Appalachia, Louisiana and the border areas with Mexico. Particular attention was placed on white music from Appalachia and African-American music from the American South. Early pioneers in musicology were mainly interested in white music, but by the 1950s a lot of African-American music began to capture attention as well. African-American music became increasingly popular and traveled to the

British Isles where it was a tremendous influence on the development of rock and rock and later rock music. In fact rock music was to some extent a synthesis of the marshal music of the British Isles and blues (not so much with jazz). As such it was not so much a deviation from existing styles of music, but a combination with new technology (amplification and instruments) and resources.

In the early stages of 20th Century interest folk music of all types and African-American music was promoted. African-American music developed more distinctly into soul music and into pop music with white performers. The African-American audience was not affluent or large enough for an industry, so promoters created a new morality for this music as a tool in breaking down racial and behavior restrictions in society, as if restrictions were wrong merely because they restricted. The overall marketing approach for popular music was class and racial mixing, and the relaxation of codes of behavior, expression of rebellion and sexual freedom. This process reached its zenith in recent years when soul and pop ultimately developed into rap with its anti-social and criminal themes. In contrast, punk music was more of a white music with similar themes, but a shorter life.

Rock and roll could be seen as ultimately developing into rock music and leaving African-American music behind except for the limited impact of funk music. The Beatles could be considered as rock and roll in their early period and rock/pop in their later period. In the early rock and roll period, they, Elvis Pressley and others attracted cult followings in addition to groupies. The cult followings displayed odd behavior such as fainting and other loss of control, such as had been earlier experienced in religious events. In the early days was claimed that the music of the Beatles and other performers had imbedded Satanic messages and caused social disturbances. As this music became more mainstream most of the earlier odd behavior disappeared and opposition to it mostly disappeared.

Proponents of rock music encouraged recreational drug use for its best enjoyment. Drug use, psychedelic art and rock music were inextricably connected especially during the 1960s and 1970s. A huge number of the baby boom generation wasted countless months and years intoxicated with drugs, art and rock music. Drugs and related art, too, became mainstream as the most egregious or public excesses of users began to appear tempered.

It is interesting that in the early stages some objections to these phenomena were raised from parents, but after a short time, as with objections to other rights movements, most objections ceased. By the end of the 20th Century use of rock music and its often morally objectionable language had become widespread in commercial marketing, and there was an absence of significant social objections to it.

The early promotion of folk music waned after the 1960s, but began to re-emerge in the 1980s as part of world music. While some folk music of the 1960s used traditional forms to promote radical political positions, world and roots music was a technique to directly challenge the integrity of traditional American culture through its music by introducing a fusion style, springing from no authentic experience. The best example of this I can think of is a African-American country music group with a Hispanic singer performing salsa-esque songs at the old time/bluegrass oriented Merle Fest in North Carolina, or Linda Ronstadt performing with a Mexican Mariachi band at the same event.

Contemporary popular music since the 1950s was used to dilute and distort existing cultural patterns. In so doing, it created a faux-culture, although it was not a true reality, since it was not related to anything other than drugs and leisure activity. Ultimately technology allowed any form, combination and amount of music to be consumed at any time, or indeed, at all times. Of course now with the Internet, file sharing and digital music devices the cost has been greatly reduced, but the amount of money, energy, creativity and productive capacity devoted to music and visual entertainment since the advent of rock and roll is mind boggling, especially when we understand that it is, in and of itself, not productive, but leisure. Moreover, this may be socially counterproductive and incapacitating leisure. How could our society afford this? Is this a social investment that will bring benefits in the generations to come. Do we benefit when we adopt slogans from social misfits (modern musicians) in place of those from direct experience, or from ancient saints and sages?

Chapter 15. The Great Suburban Boom and the New Post-World War II America

Overview

Particularly since the end of World War II the United States was the beneficiary of fortuitous and deceptive economic conditions that discouraged stable communities and local control of assets. Suburbanization was one outcome of the deceptive Post-World War II American prosperity that was supported by government policies and the availability/affordability of oil-based fuel products. Now that many Americans are beginning to see the actual weak/manipulated foundation of this prosperity, the role of a number of recent events and policies can be seen in bringing about a major social and political restructuring in America. For example, huge investments had been made in industrial facilities, urban housing and equipment in the period after 1870 until around 1950. After 1950 much of this investment was lost due to the suburbanization promoted by developers, transportation improvements and government subsidies; and by relocation from undesirable urban social and financial conditions. This change was presented as modernization or improved efficiency from new development patterns and construction, but represented a huge financial, not to mention social loss from the extensive abandonment of existing facilities.

Traditional industrial facilities and urban settlements were usually located where all sorts of urban facilities could be provided very efficiently. Even late 19th and early 20th Century suburbanization to accommodate a growing population was largely self-financed by developers and other business interests (such as electricity companies) through fixed infrastructure such as streetcars, trams and other rail transport such as commuter rail. In contrast, the pattern of Post-World War II suburbanization was skewed by construction of new public-funded infrastructure (at a higher capacity due to maturing urban standards), provision of government subsidized mortgages, and the use of private cars and radial roads.

There was definitely a basic attraction to suburban living as part of the American frontier myth. In addition subsidized mortgages and subsidized road construction provided a wealth transfer from urban residents to suburban residents. Construction, furnishings, private recreational equipment, and car sales increased substantially to fill the new spaces. Rural and semi-rural land owners benefitted along with developers and banks from massive land sale and development around urban areas. Since so much more personal and transportation space was available in the suburbs consumption increased to a new level. However, sufficient public facilities did not exist in the suburbs so they had to be built new and quickly, adding initially unsubsidized costs to suburbanization. A good example of this is the use of mobile trailers for schools. Taxes were generally lower in suburban areas due to the very lack of facilities and new facilities may have been of a better standard than those that were there before. However, taxes on the original residents were increased considerably over a short time to support the higher level of services, and increased suburban demand improved economic opportunities there in the first stages of suburbanization.

The new suburban residents were a composite of America but with generally less representation of African-Americans and Hispanics. Although the earlier American urban experience had provided modern sector jobs in areas where the workers were drawn from different groups and physical communities, in most individual communities the residential settings provided common historical, economic, religious and ethnic group support. However, in the new suburbs residents had almost no common bond other than the current consumption of goods and services. Moreover, suburban residents worked at different organizational levels, in different economic sectors and with different remuneration; came from different ethnic groups and sectarian associations, and had different historical and geographic experience. As a result, the common bonds in the suburbs were the school, public services and taxes, the mass media and consumption.

The suburban experience reached its zenith with school age children. Television, radio, newspapers, magazines, comic books, books and markets (especially malls) became the common identity of suburban youth. Even though they might have ethnic or sectarian differences at home, the common experience was largely beyond those differences which only adjusted the common experience in minor ways for most youth. Examples of home differences would be religious days, holidays, some dietary restrictions, etc, which were largely surmounted by clever marketing and product design. The common youth experience was mostly independent of home culture. External influence on the primary home culture had been observed throughout America's history, but the suburban experience inserted daily culture as paramount and home culture as secondary. This was a major change. There were some differences that sprang from the home culture that persisted, but those differences were almost invisible within the daily shared culture.

Home differences were largely denied until specific stages of life when they produced some rifts in the suburban youth culture. Examples of these are ethnic group stages of life that ultimately bring children back to their own people and tradition anytime from puberty to college, marriage, children, retirement and death. A broader rift occurred where cultural differences resulted in choices to move away from the common suburb to locations of college and career. As long as the engine of employment and consumerism remained strong, the majority of those who grew up in suburbs remained as an apparent community, and for almost 3 generations the engine was more or less strong enough to maintain this influence until new and sometimes even fundamentally conflicting cultural groups, such as African-Americans, Hispanics, Muslims and Hindus entered the suburbs.

On the surface this recent changed cultural composition had little impact on the suburban community because of the common economic, media and consumption environment. However, these new cultural groups often sought to establish group unity in order to separate themselves from the larger suburban community. This has not always been successful, but the efforts are less well known and understood than they are actually practiced. These efforts range from neighborhood segregation to culture/religion/language classes to arranged marriages. As the ethnic composition of America has changed more and more suburban youth are experiencing dual identities in dual environments, often appearing to have no conflict within each. Ultimately, however, when the engine of employment and consumerism slows, the superficial shared culture has very little strength and any hidden core culture begins to emerge. The losers in this environment are those who have no core culture, or more clearly, those who have traded or converted their core culture for the shared media and consumption culture.

To the extent that America became suburbanized, the old unity of common family experience and values became frayed. As a result, true ideology has declined, leaving the only the general and subjective issues of economic opportunity and social equity for political debate. To the extent that core ideological and cultural values have declined, political consensus has been a loser from the suburbanization process, since most family situations are now to some extent unique and share little interest directly with other families.

Still, suburbanization has provided some physical community stability in that the new communities became older communities and many residents remained in place. However, in the second suburban generation housing was often seen as part of savings, income and investment rather than as an identity and further weakened physical community identity.

It is well known that suburbanization and inter-regional migration have reduced the tax base in older built up urban areas and partially re-imposed it in newly developed suburban areas. Even if this were a straight quid pro quo where tax and population changes were balanced it would still adversely affect the older urban areas, but such a balance was not achieved. Many more public institutions and services had been built up in older urban areas than would ever be replicated in suburban areas, so the loss of any tax base in older urban areas certainly caused local economic stress. Suburbanization and interregional migration (extra-suburbanization) resulted in a reduction of the middle class in most core urban areas. In areas where the rich still lived in the core areas they also moved out, except in some of the largest urban areas. Many of the original urban inhabitants and participants in long term urban public investments physically removed themselves from those areas and exited from an implied (not individually but as a group), but not binding, contract to support those investments.

This trend was countered in a limited way by the so-called gentrification movement of middle class young adults into core urban areas. However, it is not at all clear if this will be a long term trend and whether it can compensate for or survive the financial crisis of core urban areas. In general the core urban areas reflected an increased proportion of the poor whose contributions were much less than the cost of legacy services they were offered. At the same time the more affluent began to prefer consumption of private rather than public recreation and education services, depriving the cities of at least their participation if not also their taxes. Cities countered by taxing the businesses and affluent residents that remained, but that was still not sufficient. Some cities tried to institute benefit taxes on commuters who lived in the suburbs, but worked in the core city.

Other cities annexed suburban and exurban areas through various means.

Ultimately, none of these methods could replace a dynamic urban middle class and cities have been only temporarily rescued by Federal subsidies and immigration. Most Federal subsidies are generally overlooked by the American public because they creep into the system without much direct impact or explanation. This was the case with Federal urban subsidies. Since core urban areas could not maintain their infrastructure and services and did not have the power to compel those who had left to pay to sustain them, Federal subsidies were developed for various urban sectors. The philosophical argument for an exit tax or movement control on those who are part of a long term public investment when they leave a jurisdiction is an interesting one, but goes beyond the scope of this tract. The Federal Government stepped in to provide funding and promote immigration to replace the loss of middle class residents and sustain the built up urban infrastructure. If this had not happened the infrastructure and public services would have had to be greatly reduced causing great loss to the existing plant, social upheaval and regional dislocation. This would have been the natural course of things, but it was not allowed. The cost of sustaining the previous urban status quo was subsidized by the entire country and to some extent by other countries through the Federal budget and immigration. This state of affairs was not conceptually satisfactory to any of the parties, but was an excellent short/medium term bridge solution.

As time marched on the costs continued to rise with no solution to declining taxes. During some of this period the large Federal subsidies/bailouts allowed municipal service standards to be maintained and sometimes raised as a result of temporary economic bubble prosperity, immigration and unsustainable municipal bond borrowing. Even immigration began to shift to suburban and less urbanized areas. Municipal bond funding was often justified by intellectual slight-of-hand because it should not have been used to compensate for conditions of urban decline, but rather to manage long term urban growth. At the same time that all the mechanisms for covering urban service costs had been exhausted, the bubble/international reserve currency economy and Federal financial resources began to decline. This allowed the cumulative effect of American suburbanization to be felt in direct terms. Cities such as Detroit would have to reduce even their basic services and physically remove some infrastructure plant! Yet, those cities and the entire United States tax base had been sustaining that since at least the mid-1960s! A large part of the capital investment and maintenance expenditure spent in those cities since the 1960s would now be lost!

The great railroad legacy of the United States was rapidly abandoned in the Post-World War II period in favor of road transport for both industrial and passenger travel. Just as suburbanization gave more locational and lifestyle choices, use of trucks for goods transport allowed the same expanded choices for manufacturing and commercial facility location. Because the national road system was subsidized, and the abandonment or inefficient use of rail facilities required no exit charge, considerable national wealth was also lost in this transition. This change greatly reduced the utilization of physical plant tied to railway lines, and could only be managed through subsidies and through the suburbanization and regional migration process, not through competitive costs. It was also supported through low oil and non-core land prices. Ultimately the loss of physical plant and efficient transportation was not the full loss. The subsidy of consumption (volume) instead of production (value) resulted in the expenditure of a large part of national income on extensive and less durable imported products that ultimately would have no value, and required unproductive time in their use as well as costly storage space.

In the 1960s the economic benefits of suburbanization were realized by many people at different levels from individual home owners building their own structures on their own land to small developers who prepared land for development, to builders who put their money up front in anticipation of home buyers, to large subdivision developers. The movement away from the core cities also allowed small business to take advantage of new opportunities in decentralized locations. The suburbanized environment created a boom similar in scale to that of the late 19th and early 20th Century explosion of large urban areas. Unlike that earlier robber baron environment, the suburban boom had very low scales of economic operation and was much more egalitarian. That encouraged many Americans think that the United States was truly the land of opportunity again, and that the country belonged to them. At least it seemed that way, and the new situation kept many Americans so intoxicated and occupied that they could not see what was being done in the smoke-filled rooms of technocrats and the real decision makers.

This boom and explosion of suburban opportunities was like the Gold Rush or the later Alaska Oil Pipeline bonanza - but for a much larger population all over the country. Just as in both of those environments, there was no structure in place to manage or control the broader impact of suburbanization. The United States could only ride the wave and try to stay afloat. This was a huge challenge for most communities and institutions since they had little experience in dealing with this type of rapid growth and community change.

Tremendous demands were suddenly and continuously being placed on suburban communities; and new personalities and social behavior were introduced into previously static systems. New residents found the system poorly responsive and entered community politics. At first the existing power structures prevailed, but after the first wave of development profits and with significant population and social changes, even the existing power structures became undone. In my own home town of Raleigh, North Carolina this could be seen over 40-50 years as a politically and socially conservative urban society changed into a liberal enclave in a conservative state. The means used to bring about this change was an increased and diverse population, much the same as was used in the Soviet Union and Afghanistan to control various parts of those countries.

Suburban and new growth area institutions became less oriented to the local community and more linked with the national technocratic system. This resulted in a homogeneity of operations, and ultimately of management and philosophy across the country; so much so that managers were chosen with respect to credentials and not with respect to their residence, position in the community or moral stature. This was a marked change from the 1960s when some university tenure committees reviewed nominations with respect to morals as well as academic credentials. The Civil Rights Act, and subsequent rules and legislation covered employment and participation in all but the most restrictive private activities so that traditional or local values could no longer be enforced in local institutions – institutions which were established to serve the local community! How different is this really from the Soviet commissar system?

As a long term result of suburbanization American culture became superficial and transitory. The private culture of the individual home replaced a common public culture. Vast physical plant investment was lost. Newly developed areas did not have the same density so services were fewer and more expensive (when union scales and benefits are not considered). Federal or national funding for declining urban areas replaced local funding lost by migration and suburbanization, but the cost structures of core urban areas could not adapt and net national benefits from suburbanization may have been negative, but were concealed by Federal funding, immigration and debt financing. National subsidies were hidden as part of low transportation and oil prices, international reserve currency benefits, and indirect borrowing. Immigration and gentrification provided a generational distortion to the broader pattern. Political and social cohesion of suburban America was ultimately a chimera and could only be possibly replicated by virtual communities through the Internet.

Chapter 16. Immigration and Big Population

The Nature of Labor and Wealth in the United States

The problem of labor has been evident in the New World since the days of Columbus. The scope of land and resources was vast and the immigrants generally so ambitious or greedy that other groups were always needed to achieve the development and production whose main benefit would go to the previous settlers. In short, there was an inadequate internal labor market for maximum production efficiency. Of course there were some small self-sufficient European yeoman farmers, but generally when given the chance most immigrants preferred to build on economies of scale by hiring others to work for them and to earn greater profits from the vast resources available. Much to the chagrin of the Europeans, Native Americans did not willingly respond to the settler's demand for labor, so the use of indentured European and African slave labor was introduced. This arrangement could also not supply adequate labor so the supply and low cost of labor was ultimately provided by new general immigration. In this way, population growth has been required for the American dream economy since the earliest days of the American Colonies.

The early settlers acquired wealth from possessing land and resources. Some along the coast also benefited from fishing, whaling and other seafaring activities. In the ante-bellum pre-industrial period the greatest wealth in the Colonies was probably achieved by Southerners using slave labor from the West Indies (and also in the West Indies from where a number of colonials came).

One of the most neglected issues in American history is that of labor – not of the labor movement – but of the fundamental reality of physical labor. As a result of its land conditions and climate, the South could use slave labor as a relatively cheap and effective means of production that the North could not. The North developed away from agriculture and toward trading and small industry, which was sustained by and grew from new immigration. In the South the Moravians on the Western frontier of North Carolina were an advanced German-oriented community in all aspects including technology in the late 18th and early 19th Century. The Moravians maintained a self-imposed limit on their internal community growth. As a result they found that technically, educationally and organizationally they were "top heavy" and could not generate adequate supporting labor from within their own ranks, since in America in contrast to Europe, apprentices wanted to be masters within a short time and most laborers preferred to own their own farms. There was limited immigration to that region, so to satisfy their labor needs the Moravians first turned to the mainly English settlers in nearby areas, but they found this labor unruly and undependable (and often adversarial such as when they unlawfully occupied Moravian land). The only really dependable labor they could find came from hiring slaves from English settlers.

The experience of the Moravians was only one example that shows that white labor was not naturally willing or able to do hard work, except where they had no great need or possibility for independence. Contrary to the American Myth, a large number of early American settlers were looking for an easier life rather than for an opportunity to acquire more wealth through hard work, starting from the early days of the Spanish search for El Dorado. Outside of New England, this desire for independence and easier life can be seen in the large population that settled on independent farmsteads rather than in clustered village development where greater development was possible. Ultimately since the Moravians were small in number and non-aggressive they lost their lands to occupation by others, and could not sustain themselves as an economic power in the rapidly growing America.

In contrast, similar groups in the Northeast were able to sustain themselves and increase their power for some time. Small industries in the Northeast could dominate inexperienced immigrants where land was not easily available nearby and gain the production profits that allowed them to grow in importance in the new country. Since labor could be controlled by the limited land available for settlement, the remaining challenge to the power of Northern industry was to control the price of raw materials and competing products from Europe. These challenges could be addressed to some extent by national tariffs that were harmful to the Southern States, and were to be later addressed in the War of Northern Aggression and resolved in favor of Northern industry. Not only did the War of Northern Aggression destroy the independent trading regime of the South, but it also broke the population control that was the slave economy and the only effective labor strategy for significant wealth creation. This provides a proverbial lesson. It is the control of population numbers that provides the opportunity to assert or protect a community (this was also explained to me recently in the context of family size in Afghanistan villages) unless there is another case-specific way that can remove competitors and challengers.

The institution of slavery might have been maintained in the South for many more years had the United States population not grown rapidly enough to develop low-cost labor industry in the North and provide a national army that could discourage rather than defend local independence. After slavery was abolished some people raised mild objections to the treatment of Native Americans and others about the exploitation of natural resources, but these were ultimately overpowered and most of the available benefits from the American continent were tapped as quickly and rapaciously as possible. The most enterprising, ruthless, or well connected got the most profitable assets. Since there were almost unlimited natural resources in the United States, the rich never had enough resources to capture it all, so second level assets were claimed by the masses who enjoyed unexpected prosperity until about the 1930s and the rural and small town economic decline in the latter half of the 20th Century.

Until that time, American wealth can be considered as historically remarkable in that it was largely a free windfall to the early arrivals. Early settlers could use their own energy to develop land and resources for which there was largely no competition. While in Europe and most of the rest of the world, usable land was largely all occupied, owned and priced, in America it could be obtained mainly with physical homesteading presence and a little luck, and then used to produce wealth. As a result, a vast part of the great American wealth is or was based on this land possession (or use of land) windfall.

Combined with easy possession/ownership of land, a relatively low domestic cost structure, limited regulation of the industrial sector (with the regulation of moonshiners being a notable exception) and small government well into the 20th Century provided great opportunities for free enterprise and invention. Many core inventions were developed during this period and really set the stage for American industrial world dominance. Later inventions during the regulated Post-World War II period may have been numerous and technically more complex, but were built on the core inventions that had been possible in the earlier era of near universal land ownership and which created the framework and foundation for all subsequent inventions. Even now it remains to be seen how much real value and benefit are provided by the recent plethora of convenience inventions from the consumer economy such as marketing and packaging which are themselves more akin to regulation than to production.

As the American frontier closed and boundaries were tightened in the later 19th Century, new immigrants could not get the same windfall opportunities as the earlier settlers. Perhaps this is because the new immigrants were less hardy and because of the greater distances involved. New immigrants had to first provide their labor to the urban market in order to build assets, rather than to use their labor to build on their own land assets. Although this evolving situation was perhaps less dangerous and risky than that of the frontier days, wealth creation became comparatively slower and more like the confined economy of Europe than the "exceptional" economy of the American colonial and early independence period.

As this structural change took place more attention was drawn to the growing urban areas and their politics as the means of adjudicating the allocation of wealth between capital and labor which had earlier been often united in the yeoman farmer. Starting in the latter 19th Century much wealth was made from immigrant factory labor. Unlike the mercantile and agricultural economies of frontier expansion times which were localized and of small scale, modern industrialization was of larger scale and involved many people in wider geographic areas. As a result, government regulation could determine the distribution of wealth in a large part of the urban economy and became more important and "politicized". As regulation increased the original frontier independence outlook of America disappeared since labor and capital issues had to be ultimately mediated by government rather than by individuals. This mediation could end in favor of capital through financial power or in favor of labor through voting power, or in some cases in industrial relocation to areas, such as the South, that were less affected by modern urban industrial conditions.

Ethnic and cultural characteristics of the original settlers continued to contribute to the character of regions for a long time. In this the United States is not unlike other older settled areas of the world. However, the influence of Old America's ethnic settlements began to decline after the initial coastal and middle prairie settlement periods. In the Post-World War II period this historical influence declined greatly in the face of urbanization, and the huge and diverse immigration.

The broad geographic/cultural areas of the contiguous United States are: the Northeast, the Middle Atlantic, the South, the Midwest/Central, the Southwest, and the Pacific Coast. Different conditions of wealth structure, frontier land acquisition and industrial labor, can be seen in these geographic areas. Over time the hinterland area (as regions and within regions) economy has gradually been brought into the urban-controlled industrial labor economy, but to a large extent the continuing division between those two economies is reflected in the red state/blue state divide, although the demise of the industrial economy may be pushing some formerly industrial areas into the red state camp, and the explosion of the service economy pushing some formerly red states into the blue state camp.

Immigrants contributed mightily to America. In the early years up until about the time of the War of Northern Aggression this was mainly in the form of non-urban labor (especially slaves), frontier clearing and adventure risk taking, and from the middle 19th Century into the 1920s) as more urban industrial labor and increased population in the North and Midwest for a growing continental economy (to supply and fill in open spaces). These two periods could be considered the key periods for development of the authentic domestic American economy.

In the late 19th and into the 20th Century increased communications and ease of travel combined with the new urban politics to increase an ethnic solidarity and linkage with countries of immigrant origin that encouraged immigration and group politics. Of course since the earliest days there had been similar relationships, but modern conditions made these more potent as demand for labor from urban elites (who were becoming more oriented to industry than to culture) prevented immigration controls. The country began to develop as separate urban industrial and traditional hinterland societies. In truth, America was two countries within the same national space until the Post-World War II period.

In the early 20th Century a more mature economy with the frontier largely closed found immigrants crowded into cities and working in highly organized industrial production and industrial support (organization and management including switchboard operation, typing, filing and other office support) activities. These masses also became the focus of marketing for all manner of new products. Most of these people could not aspire to the frontier dream or home ownership, but they could indulge in some instant gratification from the consumer market. This was the period of the greatest immigration in United States history prior to the 21st Century. Yet, it did not offer the asset windfall that was claimed by earlier generations. Immigrants continued to come because of the myths of American that had developed in an earlier time, but as they came and increased the urban industrial character of the United States they were themselves contributing to the destruction of those very myths. This situation continued until the Great Depression and World War II when political and economic crises temporarily stopped most immigration.

In the Colonial and Post-Colonial Periods American raw material products were exported to Europe with finished and high quality products imported back into American. Later finished and some high quality products were also exported to Europe taking advantage of American plentiful resources, low cost and abundant labor, and new technology. The new technology, better described as new inventions, was largely the result of limited regulation, low overheads and mental freedom to explore. However, by the time of the Great Depression the era of true low cost labor had passed, because the industrial work force was the only market large enough to consume the products of industrial society and had to have enough earnings to do so.

In the period of initial mass consumption and increased costs from urban labor, the modern finance and marketing system emerged with behind the scenes deception, and periodic scams and crises until the Great Depression. The volume of invention and innovation, still free in comparison to other countries, had broadly compensated for the increasing cost of labor, but mass consumption also ultimately needed new production, credit and marketing. This system relied on sales of time and labor saving devices, education, and on stable and increased future income streams. In the early period of mass marketing, purchases of longer term and tangible value goods dwarfed recreational and non-durable purchases. With reduced land availability these tangible goods were an alternate form of wealth creation.

Descendents of early immigrants were able to benefit from exploding urban industry in the form of increased demand for all products and from physical growth of urban settlement. Starting in the late 19th Century new immigrants in the North were resentful of work arrangements and began to rebel through labor organization when they had the opportunity until the benefits of organized labor essentially ended in the 1980s. The benefits of urban industry reached both urban labor and the non-urban economy for decades until labor costs became uncompetitive and foreign imports began to capture markets. The presence and high cost of industrial labor organization in the North was a big reason why Northern industry moved to the South in the 20th Century, bringing a low level industrialization with associated benefits to the South.

Limited unionization in the South and less conflict in industrial work there is probably due not to a different nature of labor, but to the new industrial employment that allowed semi-rural lifestyles where the rural economy had been destroyed by the War of Northern

Aggression. This situation reflected the fact that the high cost burden of urban labor in the North was replaced by lower cost old settler assets of land and self-reliance in the South. It can be understood that much of Northern urban assets were abandoned in favor of those in the South for a substantial capital loss in order to achieve labor and other operating savings. However, even this reduction in labor cost was ultimately not enough, and another move of industry and later customer service centers to India, China and other countries followed.

Early modern industrial conditions were based on inventiveness and hard work, and began to require some structural and policy management at higher levels (although to call this national would be somewhat incorrect) to keep the balance and maintain some basic control over common public interests. In the 20th Century, however, cleverness rather than inventiveness or hard work became the main source of success. Instead of new land to be developed, factory production to be increased or new inventions to implement, it was increasingly extension and manipulation of structures and systems, and supply of entertainment that were the path to riches. Of course there are frauds and deceptions in all systems at all times, but this new "mass economy" period had a scale and volume of deceptive far beyond all previous experience. Moreover, the new mass economy system began to introduce and encourage nebulous business concepts rather than practical production functions.

Previously, business strategy was revealed in visible actions and could be fairly easily assessed for its impact in production and profit. In contrast, as scale of operation increased, conceptual strategy could remain at the level of numerous manipulations in a system that might never be completely implemented or revealed and could provide benefits even by partial effects, as understood only in advanced systems analysis. Although from the earliest colonial days the unsuspecting had been duped into buying unproductive or untitled land; however, the players in those transactions were limited and the transactions themselves had an ending, even if a sad one.

However, with larger scales of business and financial operation, currency and market manipulation, and false marketing on a mass scale in an anonymous market could obscure the players, responsibility and even the true impacts of business and finance; and conclusive endings did not always result. This was a major change from the earlier American experience and began the process of the remaking the United States as an integrated social, business and financial system that could be controlled at a central level and would mature by the 1970s. Since the role of individuals at the local level, and the number of truly important individuals at higher levels was continuously reduced, it is not surprising that substantive civilizational history largely ended in the United States by the 1920s.

Immigration as Economic Policy

We can see that the nature of America changed largely through immigration and industrialization from the early colonial days until the Great Depression. There was little direct guidance or control over immigration by the American ideology except for a general distrust of foreigners and outsiders in general. Never did the American people speak a consent to massive immigration, but they did speak at various times in support of restricted immigration such as with respect to Germans in Pennsylvania during the Colonial period and Asians in the 20th Century. Support for immigration was almost always a political deal made by powerful economic interests, or simply due to the lack of any rules.

Then suddenly from out of nowhere, someone suggested (as is found at the Statue of Liberty) that the American ideology welcomed all the rejected of the world (give me your poor, your hungry, your whatever). That concept was largely confined to those immigrants who came in that way - not the long time settled. The idea that America was intended to be a refuge for all who are rejected by their home countries, and that the long term settled American People had a voice in that policy is one of the false American myths. Just as the Native Americans watched in horror as their homelands were invaded by wave after wave of European immigrants until they were powerless, so too has the relentless flow of immigrants over the past 100 or so years resulted in a majority population that is not of Colonial origin and imagines its experience to represent the true American ethos. As a result, a positive perception of immigration has gradually become part of the widely held holy grail of American ideology.

In fact the purpose of immigration in the modern period has been to control and manipulate the numbers of workers and consumers, and to reduce the influence of native-born and middle class Americans in national policy. Only when Japanese and Japanese Americans were interned during World War II and when immigration was largely halted during the Great Depression did so-called public sentiment apparently influence immigration policy. Maybe the public was not really involved in this, but the elites and policy makers took action in the public interest as a result of real national security (or self-interest) fears. Truly popular sentiment against Japanese in American would have resulted in their expulsion rather than detention, although there was some expulsion of Japanese as well as of Germans this was the exception and not the rule. During the Great Depression immigration was opposed by unions and disrupted by the Second World War, rather than being addressed broadly as part of the American ideology. Immediately after World War II there was renewed immigration from Europe, although not so large or heavily publicized as that which had taken place earlier. Even during that period of reduced immigration the American people did not influence the policy or the ideology of immigration.

From the time that the American Colonies were still being managed by a small group of proprietors and settler communities until nearly

149

the end of the 20th Century, immigrants were allowed into the United States not of right, but with reference to their ability to contribute and adapt to American standards and behavior, or more bluntly - to serve the demands of economic interests. Compliance with social and cultural norms was broadly enforced by civil society as well as by government. However, in the 1960s government and courts began to prohibit civil society from enforcing its standards on anyone and the 1965 Immigration Reform Act even rejected the concept of an American cultural community. Thus was the genesis of the concept of immigration rights.

The massive Post-World War II immigration began when then Massachusetts Senator Ted Kennedy heavily supported the abolition of the National Origins Formula, in place since the Immigration Act of 1924, and replacing it with the Immigration and Nationality Act of 1965. When the Kennedy brothers took control of American politics, immigration reform was a personal issue for that Irish Catholic-origin family. It is surprising that there was no public objection when President John Kennedy; his brother, Massachusetts Senator Ted Kennedy and their youngest brother, Attorney General Robert Kennedy openly worked to promote this personal program.

The Immigration and Nationality Act of 1965, also known as The Hart-Celler Act, abandoned the structure of American immigration policy that had been followed since the 1920s and replaced it with a system supposedly focusing on immigrants' skills, and family relationships with American citizens or legal residents of the United States. The Act came into effect on July 1, 1968 and together with the Immigration and Nationality Act of 1952 it forms the basis of America's current structured and formal immigration pattern.

Despite assurances by the Kennedys that this immigration reform would not upset America's ethnic balance, similar to the many claims for increased individual freedom against traditional values that have been raised since World War II, it did in fact alter the immigration pattern by opening doors to non-European nations, and changing forever the historical nature of American society. However, it is too simplistic to think that this change was solely the result of a Kennedy Irish ethnocentrism promoting their own genetic kin. Even if this were their motivation, the result of the Act was infinitely more extensive and unnecessary for that purpose. There would have been no need to bring the entire world to America just to enhance Irish immigration by a small amount (negligible in the final analysis). So either the Kennedys and their close advisors were not smart enough to understand the nature and impact of the immigration changes they were proposing, or they were extreme junior partners who made a deal with much more powerful interests who wanted to change the character of the American people. I am inclined to believe that it was a combination of both.

It cannot be coincidental that the immigration flood gates were only opened in 1965, long after the Post-World War II production boom was over and when immigration would not logically have been needed. There might have been some benefit in encouraging immigration when the United States was the leading power in the world immediately after the war (and as Europe did then for itself), but at the time of a downturn in the United States economy when innumerable domestic social and economic issues had been identified and were being addressed with new unprecedented, unaffordable and ultimately unsuccessful government programs, there was no public interest justification for increased immigration. Rather, the result of this new government immigration policy was to control labor and its price, further dilute and complicate and weaken the American middle class society and polity, and strengthen the technocratic and elite classes.

It also cannot be coincidental that the United States reached significant involvement in Vietnam (and barely avoided disaster in Cuba and Berlin to cite just the most obvious cases) at about the same time also for no clear purpose, directed by the so-called Kennedy brain trust (the qualifications for which are in the same serious doubt as for the policy wonkdom of the Clinton Era). Through the 1960s the United States was still selling heavy machinery, vehicles, military equipment and agricultural products throughout the world. Security arrangements with NATO and other organizations and countries made it possible for the United States to sell these high value products for which there was really no competition, but since there was no competition the quality and performance became ossified over time setting the stage for competition from Japan, Europe, Israel and later even by many developing countries.

In hindsight it can be seen that there were three actual objectives driving American foreign policy during this transition period. Included in these were not anti-communism (although it was claimed as one and related to the actual objectives) and not the well-being of America or the improvement of standard of living of Americans (although for much of the Post-World War II period the standard of living did improve). The three actual objectives behind American foreign policy were: to maintain low labor costs for American big business, to maintain international and domestic market access for American big business (although not necessary for American labor or American products), and to promote American big business interests through world policing and control of foreign countries. Investment in and immigration from developing countries were elements supporting these objectives. Since the three actual objectives of foreign policy were largely hidden under more attractive disguises, Post-World War II immigration policy and its impacts were kept out of public scrutiny to avoid popular opposition.

The massive immigration that began with the 1965 Immigration Reform Act should be seen as a continuation of the historical program to ensure sufficient labor supply at low cost to deal with the largely unlimited natural resources of the United States. However, by the Post-World War II period there was little unused or needed natural resource capacity. As a result immigration was largely urban, concentrated in the growing service sectors and culturally alien from the previous majority population. This new population generally found work at the cost of potential opportunities and higher wages of native born American workers. Low-paid immigrant workers could take the work of many unskilled native born workers, and also educated immigrants could compete with the native born for better paid jobs, but at lower wages and with less demands. As long as jobs were increasing, as they had through most of American history, this was not a labor problem for native-born Americans. After about 1965, though, much of the increased employment was due to the world reserve currency economic bubble which created unprecedented affluence and demand in the economy for services, and hope (or hype) to be the world services center. Unfortunately this could not be sustained as we have seen in the last decade. Now the United States faces limited employment opportunities for its citizens and the native-born now finally have to compete directly with new immigrants - and with the children of two immigrant boom generations as well.

To understand this how this situation has developed better it is necessary to review recent American economic history. Even in 1965 at the time of the Immigration Reform Act most Americans had little understanding of other countries. American was no longer industrializing, rather it was adjusting to the saturation of the pent up demand caused by the Great Depression and World War II. This adjustment had attracted thousands of Southern African-Americans and Appalachian whites to industrial centers in the 1950s, but by the mid-1960s that movement was over. By then there was less need for this unskilled labor which had resulted in urban unrest and political turmoil in previous times.

At the same time, those who retained their jobs through union power sought to continue to increase their earnings through agitation and political power in the Democratic Party. This, combined with the industrialization of Japan and the beginning of globalization, resulted in a continuous decline in American industrial efficiency. It was only the inefficient state of world transport, technology transfer and the presence of trade/distribution barriers that prolonged much of American industrial activity. As soon as these obstacles to free global trade and finance were overcome the rapid decline of the United States began.

This decline can be readily seen in the abandoned factories and housing of the extensive United States Northeast corridor where hundreds of miles of urban area formerly served by rail transportation and other fixed infrastructure is now derelict and abandoned. The myth behind this is that new more efficient and competitive facilities were built to replace those in other places, but the extensive capital loss of these concentrated industrial units was only partially compensated by modular suburban units that relied on highway-based trucking for their operation and that were not necessarily more efficient. Indeed it can only be imagined what the industrial geography of the United States would be today if high labor costs, abandonment of public infrastructure and other counterproductive policies could have been avoided. Perhaps the entire rustbelt would have been the productive China of today.

In the mid 1960s new immigration started as part of international business linkages and for university education. This was obviously in the interest of United States companies and government in extending their influence around the world in America's new role as world trade manager. However, by the 1970s, circumstances changed and the world system began maturing, changing access to and use of information and opportunity. As a result, large numbers of immigrants began entering the United States from developing countries as economic refugees to do work largely in the service sector with no apparent policy justification other than to promote ideology of America as the welcoming country and the new Rome. Through this all countries of the world would become tied to the United States through foreign remittances, social and economic relations, and strange political contacts (witness the use of Iraqi exiles in the second Iraq invasion). The obvious manifestations of the new immigration were ethnic restaurants, foreign taxi drivers, new urban ethnic enclaves, and the United States public developing myriad foreign policy interests and becoming more like the UN than historical America.

There have been many studies to determine whether immigration has a positive or negative on the economy (not considering the cultural impact) and most have concluded that the impact is slightly positive. In validating the judgments of these studies we have to consider that the cultural impact cost was not considered, that the purpose of the studies was to support immigration, the globalist attitudes and values of the study researchers and the study funding sources which also had global political and business agenda. Most of such studies are not at all complete or unbiased.

In fact, most of the jobs that new immigration created have been for discretionary services and to support the internal American immigrant economy, and did not increase America's industrial output. Many new immigrants were educated, and from highly competitive and corrupt societies, and so were attracted to the manipulative entrepreneurship sectors of the economy. Recent legal immigration to the United States has included the full range of skills from low to high, although officially it encourages high skilled labor. Skilled immigrants in the Post-World War II period have been the beneficiaries of capital investments by their own societies (and by other societies through foreign aid) and as such can be seen as a type of foreign investment in the United States, often with the repatriation of earnings. Less skilled service sector immigration can be seen as ultimately a negative factor in the economy in that it makes claims on the welfare state without producing any goods. Much illegal immigration, however, has made extensive contributions to the United States economy particularly through work in construction and agriculture, although there has been a cost in lost jobs to the native born and in the skewing of investment to new rather than existing facilities and maintenance.

Considered altogether, the public service, education, crime, and cultural costs of recent legal immigration would almost certainly add up to an overall negative impact, especially since that group has a heavy consumption of cheap imports (financed through national borrowing) and sends a portion of its money home as foreign remittances. The negative side of illegal immigration is that those immigrants are less educated, culturally alien and more likely not to pay tax. Employment taken by both legal and illegal immigrants would in a historically natural economy (non-rentier) have been taken by native born Americans.

The most amazing thing about recent immigration is the extent to which the changing nature of employment has accepted all shapes and sizes of immigrants. Call centers, research, media, even all levels of government itself, have accepted the new immigrants despite the primary function of these jobs naturally requiring the innate understanding of culturally and native-born Americans, deep fluency in American English and core commitment to common benefits of one's fellow countrymen which immigrants did not possess. The reason this can be accepted is that there is no longer a dominant common native-born American society. Such an environment is similar to a rentier society like that of the Arab Gulf States, but in America this has become more of an imperial administration than a rentier economy, and where there are almost no job categories that are reserved for the native-born and where most immigrants have the same rights as the native-born - and where many Americans believe this is correct.

How could the percentage of native-born Americans in production decline yet the economy and immigration expand? Americans were told that this was the character of an advanced economy and that the United States labor force would continue to move away from production and into services. This should have been automatically understood as ridiculous, but it built on the myths that flattered the self-image of Americans to think that they were naturally harder working, smarter and more virtuous than other people - and so they deserved freedom from labor!

How could it be that production was declining, yet wealth seemed to be growing and immigration was growing at an unprecedented pace? The answer is in two parts. First, Americans were actually renting or selling their physical, cultural, political assets to immigrants and other foreign investment. New immigrants bought existing housing and other products that enhanced the wealth of all Americans, but this was a declining windfall. As immigrants became settled they bought less excess or underused products and began to enter into competition with native born Americans for purchase of current and competitive products.

An example of this would be immigrants who bought derelict housing thereby enhancing the value of capital for native owners because there had been no native-born buyers. This was also the case with immigrant purchase of used cars, which boosted the market for them so that natives could buy new ones. As immigrants got settled, with their extended families (generally with more workers), they could better compete directly with natives for more desirable housing and cars and use those more efficiently, driving competitive prices up! So the initial economic windfall from immigrants was probably a one-time-only event and the second phase impact from immigrants probably resulted in a reduction (or possibly elimination) of that windfall through competition for the same products. However, this process could be replicated through the rising steps of consumption quality, but the magnitude of the initial windfall would rarely be repeated.

The large number of immigrants do purchase their goods in the United States, but today many of these are imported (as are many of their employees). To the extent that the domestic sales, transportation and distribution systems involve native-born Americans even the purchase of imports benefits them, but not to the extent that domestic production would. The affluent and privileged classes often mention the benefit of ethnic restaurants brought by immigrants. However, most food products used in ethnic restaurants are imported or grown by immigrants, and most employees and customers are immigrants themselves.

All this discussion could have been almost purely academic if the numbers had been small. However as time passed American society began to change as a result of the cumulative impact of immigration. As Gomer Pyle used to say, "surprise, surprise, surprise!" Only a few years ago there were a few immigrants working in random areas, but now the foreign-born population may be over 25 per cent nationally, and some of them are being elected as governors and acting as advisors to political leaders - on the needs of native-born Americans! Moreover many are becoming parents and even grandparents of American citizens. When the initial mass immigration and permanent residency began to be given in 1965 no one could imagine that immigrants would actually become an active and important part of the native-born society or comprise possibly the largest voting bloc in the country , but rather that they would remain at the fringe of society in niche positions and small numbers. But suddenly, as Gomer Pyle used to say, "shazam!," immigrants are acting either as if they were just like other Americans (are they?) or as agents for government action in support of their own special interests (home countries, societies or religions).

It is noteworthy that the decline of native-born American voters as a percentage of the national total was likely a defining factor in the election of Barrack Obama, among whose achievements is the appointment of many foreign born and children of recent immigrants to government positions and the further opening of United States borders to endlessly increasing numbers of immigrants who, regardless of their skin color, are bringing in a whole new texture of culture, completely foreign to what America's origins were when its wonderful adventure began back in 1776.

In any event, many would argue as my grandmother did, that "oh my, they are such nice hard working people and their countries are so poor!" Well, we will see about that. In fact, like their native-born predecessors, as soon as they can many of them stop being so hard working, thankful and deferential, and start acting as if they have full rights as citizens - which in fact they do! Citizens, yes, but Americans? With the advent of the dual citizenship there is less need for becoming authentic Americans because immigrants can also retain the privilege of citizenship in their native homeland, which is not an option for native-born Americans.

We have seen that there has been a historical interest in promoting mass immigration to the United States as a means of controlling labor. We can also see that now immigration is becoming a means of rapid destabilization over national culture and, as a result, control over national politics. Since the 1965 Immigration Reform Act, immigration has been increasingly promoted as a right; the result of unequal development or oppression in the world, or due to a need for more diversity in American society. As such, the practical result has been to increase immigration from groups that would most diverge from the traditional American social contract such as Hispanics, Muslims, Asians, etc. It can be seen that Europeans are not a major component of recent immigration. What justification is given for a change in the makeup of immigrants to one that damages the American social contract?

Immigration as a Part of Diversity Rights

It is interesting that as recently as 20 years ago proponents of immigration made the case that Hispanics would improve American society because they are "family-oriented." - as if caring for family is some type of special value that justifies group opportunities. Most groups and individuals are family-oriented, whether they are politically, ethically or morally good or bad, so in the final analysis "family-orientedness" is not a virtue in itself, since the orientation may be for good (to pass on good – not just any - values and traditions) or selfish (such as for demographic, political or self-aggrandizing objectives) intentions. The irony of this now largely defunct position is that those groups that are not family (nuclear) oriented, are most notably, native-born African-Americans and increasingly native-born whites. Using the same earlier logic promoting an increase in Hispanic immigration, some native-born African-Americans and whites should be encouraged to leave the country, but of course logic is not required for political games.

In the Post-World War II rights movements any cultural (or physical and now sexual) differences that could result in reduced opportunities were discounted, and any that could provide benefits (from the prevailing culture) were seen as quaint or promoted for bonus benefits (as if complementary knowledge of the prevailing culture is assumed). An example of this was the invitation to Barack Obama's father to give a lecture to young Barack's school class on being African, apparently so that everyone could think that Barack retained his "American" identity, but also gained some special African insight and character that Americans didn't have.

Support for this myth was conveyed in subtle and beguiling universalist messages that had linkages with socialist and communist rhetoric. In the early 1960s this support restarted after the McCarthy era with the songs of the folk movement through Pete Seeger; Peter, Paul and Mary and others that diminished nationalism and promoted universal humanism. The idea was that common humanity was greater than individual cultural differences, and this idea intruded into all areas of society, particularly music and movies, but soon also advertisement, religion and education.

This kind of myth and self-congratulatory thinking (like in Francis Fukuyama's <u>The End of History</u>) promoting the idea that immigrants adopted "our" rather than merely "some" values and knowledge and could function in the same way as native-born Americans spread throughout the society and business world. Employment qualification emphasis was increasingly placed on technical testing in isolation rather than on general social competence and commitment to the society, and little concern was given to the isolation of immigrants in their own enclaves after work, and whether this had any relation to the overall value of immigrant labor, especially in the service sector. As a result, the immigration rights movement became just another of the diversity rights movements.

One reason for the official and ruling elite promotion of immigration from foreign cultures is the myth that diversity is a contributor to prosperity. What evidence do we have for that? Are other less tolerant societies (apparently most others) less prosperous? We can observe that there are less tolerant societies that are prosperous and diverse; and diverse societies that are not prosperous or tolerant. What may be unique in the United States is the combination of prosperity and diversity and the assumption that this situation should lead to tolerance, not the other way around. In fact the unusual historical phenomenon is the combination of prosperity and diversity. Diversity uses up a lot more resources than homogeneity for holidays, cultural communication, etc., especially if native-born Americans need to interact with immigrants, but somehow within the

United States this does not seem to be an important consideration. We are told that this melting pot or mixed stew is a strong benefit for America (hybrid vigor?), yet the most obvious potential benefit of having so many Spanish speakers (as one important example) in the United States (legal, illegal, assimilated and unassimilated) has contributed little toward providing native-born Americans with a second language capability that they could use to improve American business opportunities in Latin America.

In reality, most of the benefits from immigrant diversity now actually go to immigrants and their children. Immigrants to the United States often parley their new status – either citizenship or green card – for improved opportunities - in their home countries - rather than for integrating into American society. For example, a green card holder could sell himself to a bride for more dowry, earn more money working in his home country, or could work in the United States Government or American business as an agent or a special resource, taking the place of a more difficult to educate and train native-born American. Most Americans would be shocked to know how many influential jobs – often policy and strategy – are held by immigrants. There are some reasons for this – drive, subsidy, education, comparative laziness of Americans, and skills that are self-defined such as coming from a certain other culture or speaking another language – reasons that have allowed millions of immigrants to settle in the United States. But the result is the same no matter what the good or bad reason - many opportunities have been lost to native-born and even long-resident immigrant Americans.

Not only can immigration in a mature society be harmful to opportunities for the native-born, but it can even undermine the basic social contract of the state. For example, contemporary immigrants to the United States (as well as to France, England, Germany, the Netherlands, Canada) claim that they should be given exemption from the prevailing social contract in the new country because of their values (or beliefs) that predominate in their home countries (and which often would be used there against the historical values of their settlement country), and on the basis of any claimed historical injustice. The basic for this is the assumption of immigration rights, the desirability of diversity or that the need for diversity is greater and more beneficial than is the social contract. This creates a new situation where terrorism and other social conflicts change from conflicts between nations to conflicts within nations, since disaffected people from various unfamiliar cultures are living together. Mobility and resentment are a powerful combo and become trends when no-one is watching.

Up until the 1990s Americans were told that immigrants wanted to come to the United States to enjoy its freedom and opportunities (read: wealth). In a change of positions (read: realities) now that our standard of living has been reduced a little over a decade later we are told that we now need immigrants to fill jobs that Americans are not educated for, or are not willing to do; to provide increased diversity and to support the welfare state for native born Americans! Apparently now the real objective is make native-born Americans a new supported minority in the United States!

The rarely held discussion of United States immigration policy focuses on the legal opportunities for immigration from various non-European countries and the supposed need for higher skilled applicants. Illegal immigration is assumed to be composed of mainly low-skilled labor. The discussion assumes that these assumptions are correct and that they comprise the full immigrant population. However, there are many exceptions to these conditions that increase the numbers of immigrants and are themselves largely disingenuous. Exceptions include those for investor, refugee, student and special work visa categories which essentially allow foreign elites, subsidized graduates and aggressive climbers to move to the United

States and compete with the vast majority of native-born Americans who are none of the above.

Immigration Rights as a Challenge to Nationality

By allowing long-term Green Card holders permanent residence, and others dual citizenship and permanent refugee status, the United States Government has converted residence and citizenship into economic tools, rather than national identity. But tools for what purpose? Long after the conditions that caused the refugee exodus of the so-called boat people, Vietnam is a booming economy and Americans, including some of those naturalized boat people, are rushing to Vietnam to do business there. It will be the same situation when Cuba and other countries open up to the world economy since many of their people are United States Citizens now and will be doing business as Americans, but with benefits from their national-origin. For example, in Bangladesh the number of members with Bangladeshi names seem to outnumber those with European names at the American Club.

Many naturalized American citizens and permanent residents live in their native countries to gain the most economic advantage, but dart back to the United States when things become unstable. In the same way, when things get bad in the United States modern immigrants could just pack their things and go back home where most of them retain families, right of return and invested savings. In the time of national emergency what will be the status of naturalized and permanent resident foreigners doing sensitive government and government-related jobs who have no native perspective and who have mixed loyalties?

We can already see the potential difficulties for national security in the number of incidents where Chinese immigrants have been found to be spying at their work in the United States for the Chinese Government. What would be the status of those who spend much or all of their time back in their home countries after obtaining citizenship or permanent residency? Would they still be provided taxpayer supported services even if their countries are enemies of the United States or if the United States were to face an economic crisis? Should the United States support naturalized citizens, including those who are citizens only by coincidence of birth on United States soil, when they engage in political or business activities in their home countries? What about the status of native born, naturalized and foreign residents that work for foreign political lobbies? Is it really appropriate for an alien or naturalized citizen to work or lobby for a foreign government or cultural interest within the United States.

Although immigration has emerged as a political issue, largely due to it being developed as one of a number of divisive rights movements, immigration itself is not really a meaningful subject. The real subjects are those of community wealth and unity - the social contract. In recent times the subject of the commons and the common weal have dropped out of the public discourse leaving only the rare discourse on community unity such as that by Samuel Huntington in Who Are We: The Challenges to America's National Identity. The community issue at hand is that of national identity and national interest. We really don't know what these interests are anymore. Who are our enemies? Are other countries our enemies or are only their leaders enemies? If other countries are our enemies is their culture or society, or just their boundaries? If conditions are so bad in a country where the leaders are enemies, how can we imagine that individuals can give their allegiance to America without endangering their families who remain in the other country? If it is other cultures that are our enemies then only those who forsake their cultures should be allowed to settle in the United States. Ironically, we meet and deal with most leaders of the world. Does that mean that they are okay as long as they stay in those countries - or just as long as they have power?

China exemplifies this issue. Is Communist China the enemy of the United States? Recently, American elites have downplayed the nature of the Chinese Government as if it is only "communist lite", or as if being communist is not opposed to the United States. Moreover, the economic success that underpins China under the communist lite government is attributed to the Confusion work ethic culture of the people themselves, yet the people are welcomed as students and immigrants into the United States. Maybe it is only the Chinese military that is the enemy of the United States, but they are allowed to have joint maneuvers/training with the United States military.

In a number of countries such as India, Germany, Israel, the Netherlands, and Switzerland a claim to current nationality or physical statehood can be made with reference to a grandparent or parent from those countries. In the United States this only extends to a parent. In the United States physical statehood is based on one's linkage to a state of residence and was reinforced by values and laws specific to the states under the government structure of the Republic. While much of this structure remains, federal intrusions to preempt and supersede individual state laws are well on their way to removing native-born claims to any specific location identity and rights. The ultimate destination of current trends is clear; instead of citizenship being a right of an individual's state identity, it is a gift from the Federal Government.

The silliest bases for statehood is found in the United States where the coincidence of birth on United States soil is justification for citizenship. This is now combined with the national respect for the independent claims of all other countries (internationalism) on individuals who are citizens or residents (legal and illegal) in the United States that allows special privileges such as dual citizenship and consular representation to certain individuals. The result of this policy for the United States is that the more bound a person is to the

United States by birth, parental and grandparental linkages and lack of other conflicting linkages, the more that person is disadvantaged in comparison with immigrants and children of recent immigrants. Even employers can now be seen to seek persons of foreign birth and linkages in preference to the native-born.

In contrast to this disadvantage of the native-born within the United States, contemporary international politics has emphasized the rights of original "native" peoples around the world which have been promoted above those of more recent native-born (immigrant) people in the same country because of some injustice or dislocation at a particular point in time. The claim is generally made that a current group (such as Afrikaaners, White Rhodesians, etc.) that has dispossessed a previous group must make restitution. However, the status of the previous group (wandering Zulus) is not questioned. It may be that they, too, dispossessed another group, but claims logic does not extend to that condition. No claim is made that ethnic Prussians who left Poland after World War II should return there. If a group was forced or chose as a minority to settle in the land of others, such as South Asians, Chinese, Jewish Israelis or African-Americans, no claim is made that they return to their original homelands. Ultimately the special rights claims of indigenous peoples are mainly valid then they are made against a European people; and self-determination claims where they do not conflict with geopolitical interests. For example, the Southern United States wished to secede, but were not allowed. The Kurds, Tibetans and Eastern Turkestanis want their own state, but are not allowed. Jews wanted a state where they had not had a significant presence for centuries, but were allowed.

Big Population and the New World Order

Americans were historically encouraged in to have large traditional families, but by the 1970s were warned that more than 2 children per family could not be sustained. By around AD 2000, after more than a generation of following these prescription, Americans were told that their society could not be sustained financially or technically without a net population growth which could only come from immigration from different cultures, and from both the better as well as the less educated. What happened to the concern for the population bomb of the 1970s and for encouraging traditional native-born families in the 1950s and 1960s! Now, ironically, conservatives and traditionalists, many of whom believe there is no world population crisis, will lose everything in this recommended situation. Of course this change in immigration policy is a crisis physically and culturally for the vast majority of the native-born. However, there is no immediate crisis for the elite or the poor, only for what remains of the middle class. Sometime after 1970 the problem of over-population ceased to be considered a problem for both rich and poor countries, in spite of all the management, social, environmental and political problems that it causes. Instead it was converted into the problem of global warming. How could this obvious intellectual sleight of hand have been so widely accepted?

Increasing economies of scale and globalist forces have separated from physical place and traditional group culture, and new elites are no longer bound to and controlled by localized population and culture. At the same time concern with unprecedented population sizes has almost vanished. It has been noted that as recently as the 1980s the number of people living exceeded all those who had previously died throughout history. Until our present time all institutions of government and economy have been based on some degree of historical span of control and on personal interaction that had a historical basis. Today, the historical scale has been exceeded, and the current population scale and the ambition of those controlling the political economy and government has reached unprecedented levels. Now it is impossible for government or almost any institution to retain an accountable or even human scale. That frees both government and institutions from the larger society and physical environment in the same way as the power elites have been freed. Communication is increasingly conducted in cyberspace with reference to guidelines and regulations devised by and for the benefit of unaccountable functionaries. The scale of human settlement, activity and services is no longer manageable by the old systems born of the broad society, but only through power elites and their neo-elite technical managers.

Concern with population size is largely a modern social welfare and urban issue because a higher level of first hygiene and then other social services were understood to be needed for communities where large numbers people live in close proximity to each other. Capacity to provide for limited urban areas had mostly been achieved by the 1960s when it became clear that the world would eventually become almost completely urban. Although the cost of providing services for endlessly expanding populations cannot be met, concern about population size and growth has shifted to population management rather than control. Something fundamental has changed in the total disregard of the source of mankind's greatest challenge: population. The reason for this is that population provides tremendous benefits to a powerful few in the form of consumers, workers (including soldiers) and voters (including political supporters). Now the subject of debate is not how to control the total population numbers, but where the population should live, what they should do and how they should relate to their economic and political rulers.

In contrast to the more elegant population management, cruder population exploitation is as old as the human race. Population exploitation focused historically on harnessing the maximum power of population for production. The challenge of this was how to get maximum output with minimum coercion. Populations that were free and that could unite were hard to control. As a result, they had to be divided and oppressed in various ways in order to get their output at little cost for the ruling class. It is only in recent times that a more equal distribution of benefits has been available to the masses; first privately obtained by emerging trading classes and later provided to larger populations by governments under the guise of social development. It may be that these modern urban services were needed not really to improve conditions of the population, but to control them and breed them for different conditions and technology.

Even in recent times in "democratic" France, the open public space urban planning of Haussmann that influenced British Colonial and even Washington, DC urban design was based on population exploitation (elimination of defendable community enclaves and establishment of transportation systems that enable large scale mechanized police/military control that was later expanded at a national and international scale in the United States through the Interstate Highway System and other transportation linkages and impacts).

While one of the myths of America is that of independent, self-directed and self-interested labor, in fact the American as well as the world systems have been striving with increasing speed to integrate and control larger sizes of labor by bringing larger populations into the integrated modern urban economic system in order to reduce costs and increase the market for products, including information. This results in more production at lower cost, monopolistic production and increased consumption which provide increasing power to the elite (particularly with the dislocation of technology, assets and elite allegiances). In addition, increased population provides larger resources for army, police and vote manipulation. All these aspects of increased population provide benefits to the controlling elites while diminishing the relative power of the non-elite, particularly the middle class. This explains the recent trend of American power elites having diverging interests from the middle class in particular.

As power elites were de-coupled from their peoples and nations they could look to the total potential gain from the control of large blocks of voters, consumers, soldiers and workers. Elites no longer need to worry about their relationship with the masses. They also do not need to be concerned about problems in the relationships of the masses with resources and culture since increased disparities don't affect the power elite. As a global production and consumer culture has developed, large and heterogeneous populations have become useful for those who can control them in the form of consumers, manipulated and disunited democratic citizens, and military/security manpower resources.

Within individual countries increased disunity and competition for resources among the masses has benefitted the elite through decreased mass political opportunities and consumer alternatives. The masses rarely have an opportunity to affect substantial political economy decisions because technical and localized political decisions have been atomized and taken out of the broader ideological platforms which are controlled by the elite. Moreover since the masses have little community solidarity as well as less non-work time and money, participation of the masses in policy level politics (even if the policy is not coherent) has declined. This process is furthered by pitting the middle class against the poor, the entitlement classes (supported by government and institutions) against the productive classes (supported by direct market-related work), and various special interests against each other within the middle class. As a result there is almost no structure or definition of the conflict between the power elite and the masses, and particularly of that between the power elite and the middle class.

At the global level increased population and disunity within countries provide an additional level of competition and distraction that further dis-empowers the non-elites. With the exception of a just a couple of countries like North Korea, the power elite that control the communications and markets of most countries have been educated and indoctrinated in American and European political, market and management philosophy. The core elements of this are the so-called free market economy and popular political elections. Both of these, separately and combined, increase the opportunity to divert the attention and diffuse the power of greater numbers of people both nationally and internationally, so that the small number of focused elites can pursue their agenda with limited transparency, resistance and regulation.

The methodology of large scale population management and manipulation within countries can be seen in examples as diverse as the mixed communist population control and pseudo-capitalism of Red China, vote-block politics in India; red, blue and swing state demographics, special rights movements and the election of a mixed ethnic president in the United States; and most recently the migrant crisis in Europe. These and many other demographic, economic and political developments around the world do not represent successful democracy or free markets, but the management and manipulation of large populations. If we view current global developments and news from this perspective rather than from the analysis of individual factors independently, we can see that the central issue is management and manipulation of large populations which ultimately have no natural limit.

Dominance of the modern industrial sector was one of the advantages that allowed the United States to maintain great prosperity and economic mobility. However, as American technology has been shared with other countries the industrial sector and its importance to the American political economy has declined. It was thought that this would simply mean that more products would be imported from other countries and that Americans would increasingly work in non-productive sectors where the United States would be similarly dominant and competitive.

Services (including marketing and supply of goods), education and technology have emerged as the economic growth sectors, but these are not great physical prosperity engines. Since, unlike in the traditional industrial sector, there is limited formal social control over these sectors it was assumed that under increasingly open market conditions with numerous rights group claimants there would be increased domestic economic leveling within these sectors (as by extension within the entire American society). Surprisingly leveling around the middle class has not resulted since middle class opportunities have greatly decreased. Instead the leveling is taking place mainly at the lower economic levels of society. Americans now face competition for decreasing domestic opportunities from a constantly expanding number of people in every country in the world whether they live in their native countries or immigrate to the United States.

The beneficiaries of this emerging scenario are clearly those who can control - or help control - "big population". Secondary and possibly temporary beneficiaries are those who can claim institutional entitlements, and immigrants who can vertically move up the economic ladder within the same profession by claiming shares in the established United States economy in exchange for shares in a less rewarding economy. The obvious loser is the "great American middle class" which has long driven the progress of modern civilization and ethics.

Chapter 17. The American Economy and the Rentier State

Overview

Previous chapters have explored the unique nature of the United States history and society. In particular we have seen that the United States was a large area of land with vast resources that allowed all classes to achieve unprecedented "windfall" prosperity with limited conflicts among themselves until the mid 1800s. From that time onwards regional and class conflicts increased continuously through the War of Northern Aggression, World War I, the Great Depression and World War II. Yet despite these traumatic events, by the 1950s and early 1960s American prosperity was miraculously greater than ever and towered over the rest of the world.

 Yet, this situation was mostly due to passive rather than active collection of benefits arising from conditions in the rest of the world and the still vast domestic resources which were greater than the available capacity to capture them. Yet, propagation and acceptance of positive national myths (of hard work, virtue and intelligence) led the nation to believe that its capacity remained unlimited. As a result programs to share resources and power within the national population and the world community were embraced on a complete and continuous basis. There seemed to be no benefits that could not be provided, rights that could not be extended and enlarged, and comfort that could not be made available.

Yet, slowly the economic and political noose tightened, but Americans thought increasing struggles were only temporary and could be overcome in order to return to the level of past prosperity. The financial crises of the early 21st Century have brought together all the economic, social and political contradictions of the Post-World War II world reserve currency-based American financial mirage. Once the fog began to lift many people began to open their eyes and consider new logical, but heretofore unorthodox explanations for much of their reality. As a result the American myths began to come undone and the popular concept of American Exceptionalism could no longer be defended. Unfortunately, President Obama is right when he suggests that Americans are not much more exceptional than are other people - but it is not because Americans are not unique, which they are, but because they are not so unique as is their response to the unique American experience.

If we put aside the broader issues of the global financial system (in particular, of direct international borrowings by the United States) for the time being and only focus our attention on the domestic side of finance and the economy in the United States we can see that even conditions and developments that are and have been within direct domestic control are already having disastrous and unprecedented consequences.

Since World War II many directly productive asset classes such as workshops, factories, labor, even some land gradually lost their value (a good example of this could be seen from a trip by train from Boston to Washington, DC passing by derelict buildings worth billions). How could the United States afford to lose these millions of industrial square feet? The answer is that the United States over a brief period of years converted from a production to a consumption economy.

When we look back at the 1950s and 1960s and 1970s we can see the gradual disappearance of the Honeymooners and the emergence of Three's Company. All of a sudden instead of producing, lots of people were doing service jobs and just consuming. I remember some of the last traditional white sharecropper farmers in Wake County, North Carolina. They lived a poor, but decent life into the 1970s. Then suddenly they were gone and their land was sold for non-productive purposes. We didn't think anything of it then, but some people noticed the loss of so many traditional patterns and activities. All of a sudden those patterns and activities didn't or couldn't function any more. Traditional crafts and products also vanished and were replaced by cheap imports. That was the birth of the American consumption and leisure society. Who did we know that actually worked in production? Well my aunt and uncle still worked in factories into the 1980s, but they were the only ones in my whole circle of friends and acquaintances. In the place of the productive labor of the past, now many young people had the freedom, wealth and time to get high on drugs and protest about Vietnam. As we became further removed from reality, so did our discipline and morals as we turned our backs on all traditional values and patterns that are largely followed by the rest of the world outside of Europe.

As American production competitiveness declined there was a shift in investment and savings to consumption (increasingly of short lived and non-physical products including computer software), and to housing, equities and financial instruments (sometimes to reduce tax liability). *Unfortunately, because of the decline of physical production (and of its associated physical plant) the economy came to rely increasingly on immigration for consumption of existing assets, lowering labor costs and expanding consumer demand (this can be considered a form of foreign investment in the United States); as well as to rely on direct American investment overseas where returns were greater.* If there is any confusion about the way population growth affects broad social wealth the reader is encouraged to read Henry George's Progress and Poverty - from 1838!

One key force behind the industrial decline of the United States is *alienation of control* – political, legal, social, financial and economic power from the great middle class. We have already seen how political and economic alienation was achieved from the earliest days of the American Republic in the Whiskey Rebellion, the War of Northern Aggression and the dispossession of Native American land. We have also seen how social alienation has taken place through various rights and immigration policies. Further alienation has taken place through the establishment of government as a market force, as a regulator and by the development of a national caste system for co-called professional activities.

Government as a Monopolistic Business

The value of the common production and assets of a nation or a geographically defined political and social entity are not all the result of direct efforts of the owners and occupiers. As explained by Henry George in his classic <u>Progress and Poverty</u>, initial ubiquitous resources, principally land, distributed equally eventually begin to acquire additional unearned values as a result of their relational location to population and development (ideas related to the brilliant work of von Thunen and his central place theory). In recognition of this George proposed public ownership of land and a single tax, or rent on it, to capture the common wealth.

When I was a child I thought that there was a large public service component in the economy something like expropriated labor or corvée, which is the norm in history. I imagined that when the government needed things urgently such as soldiers and equipment these would be provided by individuals and producers either free or at a low cost in the public interest. In fact this continued in the United States in the form of the military draft until 1973 and in the continued more limited tradition of jury duty. Now there is hardly any memory of shared and obligatory public service for more than two generations.

My parents explained to me that government was just another customer and had to buy in the market. That didn't satisfy me, but as I grew older it seemed to be true, although somewhat illogical. Probably the reason for this new role of government as a business was the substitution of regular taxes for periodic levies under the United States 16th Constitutional Amendment in 1913. Essentially this meant that government would be independent and automatic in its activities rather than episodic and dependent on the public concurrence and contributions. This has certainly had a major impact on the relationship between government and the people, since government can actually take many decisions without public consultation and can develop ongoing activities without direct public authorization; submitting the bill after the expense is incurred. Of course it is theoretically possible to defund programs and reverse administrative actions through the legislative process, but in practice this is almost impossible.

With the establishment of the income tax, not only is there no conscription of goods and services by the government – but also there is now even greater profitability for large corporations working in the government sector than for those in the private sector as a result of the limited competition in the government sector. This was suspected during the glory days of World War II when business giants obtained special non-competitive contracts with the government, but it has become institutionalized in recent years as a result of the privatizing of government work; which is particularly evident in Iraq and Afghanistan. The specialized nature of government contracting and operations makes government work different from that in ordinary markets. As a result, specialist firms and individuals focus their energies on the government market where competition is less due to restrictive characteristics. As a result of the shift in importance of production and consumption centers to regulation and procurement centers (political capitals), it should not be surprising that in 2014 five of the ten wealthiest jurisdictions in America are in the Washington Metropolitan Region.

A high level of government services was achieved by government in the guise of public service through the income and later additional social benefit taxes. However, in recent years there has been an insidious trend of mixing the earlier role of government as public servant with its new role as monopolistic business through the introduction of new charges for parks and other public services that have been paid for, or should have been paid from, taxes. Even more disturbing is the belief by those coming up with or implementing such charges that it is a great discovery and public service - as if it they are inventing revenues out of thin air or discovering a lost treasure.

Service charges have proved to be a useful financial technique in developing countries where taxes are very inadequate. Even in my own professional work I have helped introduce community financial contribution for local development in India and have observed this approach increasingly encouraged by international agencies. However, American taxes have traditionally been sufficient because they were linked and limited to the cost of government services. What has changed in the United States is the introduction of a system wide deception with respect to the actual services provided and costs incurred, and the encroachment of government into the traditional domain of private business. If tax revenues were not sufficient for public services then the services should be reduced or taxes raised, rather than adopting a hybrid system of using taxes to set up an institution to provide services, and then using extra charges to fund operation. The impact of this structure goes much beyond that coming from the military-industrial complex which Eisenhower warned about.

The concept of private sector insider trading is generally understood by most people. Indeed it has become so pervasive and unpunished at the higher levels that it hardly merits headlines these days. Less known and understood is the incredible monopoly power that government has acquired over public resources and space. Government regulation and contracting constitute a much greater and more insidious form of insider trading than that found in private business because private business always has some uncertainties, but government rarely does since it makes the rules and officiates the game. There are numerous examples where government regulatory monopoly provides support and subsidy to the rich, particular in finance and real estate development. When I was in city planning graduate school one of my professors said that he did not know of any case of a major shopping center development application being turned down, whereas small development applications are routinely rejected.

Since there are limited business opportunities and scales of economy for certain types of activity and development such as accessible real estate, shopping centers, airwaves, cable television, advertising on public transportation, military equipment, security services, and logistical support, regulation and sale of the use of public space ensures monopolies by creating artificial markets not unlike the historical natural monopolies such as electricity supply and public transportation. The income obtained from these activities is normally used not to defray existing costs or to provide specific new public benefits, but as new revenues (taxes) and power un-ratified by the public. Those who dream these things up, such as students in planning school, think themselves geniuses for coming up with such arrangements, but give no thought to the intrusion into private space from this extension of already tax-payer purchased public space.

Diminished Performance of Hybrid Government

The emergence of a hybrid entity with characteristics of both the public and private sectors has been a hugely destabilizing force for the historical American political economy. There is reduced quality in the government work due to procedures and specifications that are more bureaucratic than technical; but, there are even more obstacles to achieving good value for money in government sector contracting. One such obstacle is the presence of policies that attempt to achieve social or political purposes through the modification of technical requirements. An example of this is the incentive given to companies owned by the disadvantaged/minorities (defined without discussion of whether they should be deserving as privileged company owners, whether and which minorities should be given any assistance, or whether their employees are themselves minorities or otherwise even qualified).

In addition to such contract preferences, government employment itself is a vehicle for promoting social policy goals. This means in practice that there are those in government employment that do not meet the requirements for open competition, and who will oversee contracting to companies and individuals who are chosen based on social policy rather than performance criteria. After nearly 50 years of this affirmative action system, where so-called equity and representation trump competence, the cumulative effect is felt in a diminished overall performance of the system. Moreover, the poor quality of the system now reduces even the number of qualified companies, products and individuals who might want to work in it, or with it. At the same time security and benefits of those jobs increasingly diverge from those of the non-government related private sector.

A second obstacle to getting value for money from government is the contracting of services on a project and immediate need basis. Such contracting is time bound and has no long-term obligations. As a result, extensive institutional memory of the actual work (as opposed to that of the contracting or the contracting procedure) is lost. Much contracted work will have to be repeated each time one contract ends and a new one begins. Anyone who has experienced such a transition would understand that this is a fact. As from the use of government for social policy, the cumulative negative effect on government performance from the use of contracting is beginning to be felt, although the extent and length of experience is less than that with affirmative action.

Initially contracting was advocated as a cost effective method of providing services, but this was based on the flawed assumption that sufficient funds would be available to complete contract work, maintain it and build directly on it with follow on contracts or continuous in-house collaboration. This has largely been an unfulfilled expectation for many reasons. The result has been that most new and updated work also requires reconstruction of previous work. Normally this cannot be done since those knowledgeable of that work are no longer available. Often justification for hiring the company that did the original work is made on the basis of maintaining continuity, but in reality the actual individuals who did the work are not actually available! The current system of contracting and consulting cannot succeed. Instead of contracting to private business, permanent individuals of quality are needed to serve in the public interest, but the new form of hybrid government does not attract them.

The Incredible Expanding Domain of Government Control

Prior to the late 20th Century, except in a few large urban areas, wealth was created locally and the local rich depended in part on the economic surplus of local labor and materials. Local wealth was a result of labor and materials, but also to some extent of capital and skills. In the United States some areas and communities which had not developed in comparison with others were identified in the Johnson Administration's "War on Poverty," under which the government sought to continue New Deal type programs even during generally prosperous times. This establishment of permanent government activism was a precursor of the permanent war on terrorism which was established by George Bush after September 11, 2001.

Treating poverty as a social problem to be addressed and subsidized by government created a class of people that depended on assistance and a class of those providing that assistance. The lack of debate about a reasonable income distribution, the role of class in society, the nature of honest achievement and the consequences of fraud and malfeasance allows a subjective definition of poverty which could include almost everybody, as evidenced by the current movement against "the 1%," implying that 99% could be disadvantaged.

At the same time as assistance to all disadvantaged groups became more extensive and their lives more comfortable, community wealth became less dependent on production and capital. Capital began to seek locations where it was more productive, and ultimately this led overseas where there were few if any safeguards comparable to those in the United States. As capital and wealth depended less on the local community there was reduced symbiosis between capital and labor, and reduced community identity. Taking the place of local productive capital were the government entitlement providers who prospered with more clients and greater services. This process of government activism even expanded to foreign assistance. With no relationship to community or production, domestic and foreign welfare became two of the main growth sectors in the economy funded by autonomous government budgets.

In the United States and Western Europe the size of the entitlement claiming and delivering classes has now become so huge that it is no longer possible to generate the revenues to cover this from the formal domestic economy. Profits from foreign operations and from undocumented domestic labor also contribute to the cost of this welfare state. Maybe that is why those two sectors of the economy have grown so large. One problem in this scenario is that repatriation of foreign investment profits is declining and the social cost of undocumented workers increasing. Moreover, overseas profit repatriation can only benefit the country at large if it is distributed widely as investment earnings or from taxation. Unfortunately, only a small portion of household income is from dividends and the actual repatriated profits are not large enough to support the large unproductive components of the welfare economy.

As the government has increased its regulation, participation and control over many economic and business activities the corresponding response by the business sector has been largely ignored. Far from government and business being adversaries, government and big business have worked in a complimentary way to dominate and control other stakeholders in the society. Corporations and multi-nationals represent larger scale business and have used the power of government to prohibit the entry of most other stakeholders through patent, copyright and corporate protection under the law.

Patent, Copyright and Corporate Protection

In the early years of the United States many benefits were obtained from the use of primary patent protection, but there were probably more benefits from unprotected secondary than from protected primary inventions, although the myth is that primary inventors are the most important and would only sacrifice their time and energy in order to gain secure rewards facilitated from patent protection. Even with patent protection many authentic inventors were cheated out of their benefits by more clever individuals or powerful companies. This can be seen as a continuation of the desire to get rich quick, or to control the market by restricting competition. In any event, patent protection for products or techniques expanded into copyright protection for ideas and identity.

Concepts of ideas and identity are the domain of the artistic field, broadly speaking, and protection of these allowed for the potential to capture and package almost any idea or expression for private gain; again rewarding the clever rather than the hard working and creative. Most ideas and expression are not new or unique. It is only the cleverness in capturing and packaging that give them a market and value. So-called intellectual property is itself a type of myth. If an individual or company can claim an idea or product, they can capture fees for potentially unlimited periods. There may be some justification for providing protection for invention of products and techniques, but otherwise for most people in ordinary life rewards are normally episodic and limited in the short term and become significant only as they accumulate over the long term.

This demonstrates an aspect of American culture where clever planning and manipulation are better rewarded than dependability and hard work. The environment and impact of this are suggested in the book, Winner Take All Society by Frank and Cook. That book discusses how the nature of rewards in contemporary American society encourages some people to be single minded only for acquiring top positions and power, since there are only two broad levels of rewards: subsistence and windfall. This further separates Americans into the haves and have-nots. Basically patent and copyright protection enlisted protection from the government for newly defined private property claims rather than for hard work and sacrifice.

In a way similar to patent and copyright protection, the establishment of a legal basis for corporate identity as a pseudo person, was a means of using government to shield the assets and actions of individuals from liability claims of other individuals. A corporation is not the individuals that own it or work for it, as a partnership would be, but a legal individual whose identity is separate from any of the owners of workers. Individuals acting under the shield of a corporation cannot be held personally accountable for many of their actions. The same is true in much the same way for government employees. Thus, for many clever and smart individuals, it is wise to seek the security of corporate and government employment, rather than to live and work as an insecure responsible individual.

Corporate identity has many legal, economic and social implications. In a nutshell, in a corporation actions of humans become shielded by the law. As a result, many of their consequences cannot be felt, regulated or punished by normal society, since they become legal rather than ethical or social matters. An example of this would be that of specific individuals employed by corporations and their actions responsible for losses of investor savings due to fraud. Since these individuals are shielded by corporations, and many may not even be personally identified for their individual acts, it is difficult to identify them and take direct action against them. As a result many of these guilty individuals are still living lives of comfort and affluence from the profits of Enron, the Savings and Loan Scandal and other frauds. As the full potential of corporate power has been secured with restricted liability and taxation; regulation that is onerous for smaller stakeholders, and though monopolistic practices and economies; accountable non-corporate community, public and private investment has been greatly reduced.

Consumerism as Pseudo Economic Production

For a long time consumed products *reflected and supported* aspects of experienced and authentic American culture; even as fads. However, sometime in the 1970s and 1980s, consumerism *became* American culture. The time required for actual culture was reduced by the availability and substitution of faux-culture. By the time of Ronald Reagan' election most Americans had adopted the myth that being American was defined by the desire to participate in the consumer economy and the chance to get rich. Strangely that myth became the main Republican argument for continued immigration because ambition and consumerism did not need to be restricted to native-born Americans. That myth became the basis for the current Republican ideology of American Exceptionalism. Ironically, a few years later, the same myth was promoted by the Communist Chinese for its own citizens in the form of, "its glorious to be rich".

Naomi Klein alludes to one element of consumerism in her book, No Logos, in that product branding is not the same as the actual product characteristics and can even be extended into a lifestyle concept. However Klein does not take the next logical step to the understanding of this branding as a method of broader social and political myth creation. In the Post-World War II period national fads and propaganda advertising shaped many perceptions which were used to promote social as well as commercial myths. These myths are only one component in the system of the American political, cultural and commercial brands. The active presentation of situations or images that are distorted, taken out of context or patently wrong, creates myths that are accepted as the basis for decisions and judgments on related issues, without direct consideration or validation of actual behavior. As a result social agenda and propaganda can blend into manufactured and manipulated image and concept myths in the same way that marketing campaigns create lifestyle myths.

Not Really Globalization, but Business Freedom from Place

Ultimately the key objective of modern business is market control either through propaganda, restrictive regulations or monopoly. We have already seen that the Whiskey Rebellion was ruthlessly put down by George Washington in order to establish government revenue. Moreover many government policies toward homemade liquor, tobacco, and other food production and technology have obviously been developed to promote institutional business and economic interests at the cost of private rights. As government and regulation, and economies of scale have expanded, the distinction between the public and private sectors has blurred or even vanished.

What remains is the distinction between those with money and power and those without.

The American perspective on "economic" (a much over- and misleadingly- used term) national interest has been distorted in recent years to promote "business" rather than "the economy". This is a very important change since the interest of "business" is not the same as the national or common "economy". This change to the promotion of business over a common economy requires acceptance of modern capitalist objectives and patterns of consumption and growth such as capital and labor mobility. At first it seems that this might be a good thing such as letting capital and labor move to the places where they can yield the most for the greater efficiency and benefit. Unfortunately, this is just a sugar-coated way of giving capital freedom from place. Since everyone belongs in a place, freeing business from place means that unless your place is receiving business, it is losing it. In most of America's historical experience, freedom from place meant that opportunities were coming **to** your place so you could expect to benefit. In some cases where opportunities were leaving your place, the new place was just being built or expanding and moving from your place to a new place was also likely a good opportunity for you as well.

Modern business argues that new or preserved opportunities require unrestricted disturbance of the natural environment by equipment of unlimited destructive power. Since most American business was physically restricted to the United States economy most people ultimately acquiesced to this unrestricted environment since there was a reasonable expectation that the costs would also have greater benefits for the local or at least the domestic economy. However, with the establishment of the multi-national corporation, previous local environmental costs could no longer be justified since business was not captive to the domestic economy and could transfer the benefits to other places. Minor short and medium term cost savings possible for business in other places (and countries) could justify relocation even after local communities had made costly and irrevocable long term physical investments. In practice, freedom from place has meant the massive wastage of government and community infrastructure and spending that is lost when businesses moves for their individual and independent short and medium term benefits.

Initially, globalism and international market expansion were welcomed when this appeared to mean improvement in national American wealth, but increasingly this globalization meant corporate wealth, but national loss. The current global business environment with limited restrictions on location and capital is such that large scale mobility of knowledge, plant and labor makes domestic management of economic infrastructure by the nation difficult. As a result, business practices and ethics respond to the lowest margins and standards, so that most of the large scale business (and there is very little small business remaining) economy are no longer responsive or accountable to the public. For example, is it reasonable that the United States needs Indian labor both in the United States and in India to sustain the computer and software industries, despite the fact that these industries were founded and developed by native-born Americans and while India has otherwise not been able to become a developed country?

Recently I visited a jute weaving factory in a remote district in Bangladesh; an industry that I thought was mostly defunct. The nicely buzzing factory was filled with almost all young women operating a range of machinery. Some of the women were typical dull factory workers just putting in their time, but quite a few were talking and smiling as they worked. Despite their low wages they all wore colorful clothes and many wore simple jewelry. I wondered how this would have compared to similar American factories half a century ago. I think our people would have been less thoughtful in their dress and maybe less happy. Maybe it has something to do with their attitude of getting on with living rather than thinking about social injustice. No safety features or clothing were visible and the dust must ultimately have a bad effect on them. When I was leaving the manager told us that except for the last stringing machines, all the other machines were Chinese. There you have it. Machinery makes the world go around - not IT and financial slight-of-hand. The West invented it. The Chinese make it. Americans think that we don't need to manufacture or sell products because we are better educated and can do higher level work. But, since technology is location-agnostic and management is standardized, if wages are low enough, training can be provided to anyone anywhere and production will move there. As long as production is achieved there is some real value to someone somewhere. Levels of education and local sensitivity are proving to be of little importance in this environment.

The non-production-based markets which now dominate the United States economy behave differently. Since much of their value is only on paper rather than in physical or actual products, it cannot be recovered at the time of various financial crises and scams, but can only be shown on paper accounts. Clever and sophisticated accounting practices have been increasingly used to show often conceptual or fictitious *earnings* instead of actual *sales profits*. Once accounting earnings and capital gains profits can no longer be fabricated, joining long lost production profits, there are few options left that would yield authentic earnings to capital in the United States.

In hindsight it is hard to believe that the United States was willing to fund the Marshall Plan when it was ultimately possible for Europe and Japan to be more than restored (and maybe superior to the United States) in less than 20 years? Was it really in the interest of the American people to support that strong international competition which ultimately damaged their own well-being? Or rather, was the purpose to subsidize privileged American investors (not ordinary Americans)? The results speak for themselves. The same question can be asked about normalizing relations with Red China? Was it to improve world peace or to free the Chinese People from an oppressive government? Or maybe it was because the American market potential had peaked and big business investors needed new facilitation in China for world profits? Under the new economic relations regime with Red China the United States lost most of its production capacity and only retained military, consumption and reserve currency importance. Again, the results speak for themselves. Is it any surprise that since World War II the United States has supported great military investments, sales and interventions, but that the benefits from those have been both limited and restricted. In contrast, emphasis on the military sector has led more to huge costs to the public from deaths, injuries and medical treatment.

In addition to the Post-World War II trade in military services, the United States also shifted from sales of products to sales of assets. Assets that were sold were technology, education, residency, engineering, materials, branding and technical advice. The American people did not get the direct benefits from these asset sales since ordinary people were not the owners. Ultimately sales of assets are not of a continuing nature, but necessarily diminish over time, since they are the source of wealth production. Those asset sales were the first round of economic and political structural loss to the United States and will turn out to be the most destructive, but they did not result in the final loss of American sovereignty. However, they set the stage for the loss of national sovereignty in combination with the social and physiological damage to the middle class that has been described in previous chapters.

The End Game – Mature Capitalism

In the mature economic and financial system in the United States, a very large part of national capital is really "accounting capital" and not actual money or physical assets. This accounting capital has been growing much faster than productive opportunities and the results are manifest as an increase in the money supply, in a reduction in profitable investment opportunities and at the same time, deflation in the prices of many goods and services. This appears counterintuitive since increase in money supply would indicate an increase in the prices of goods, but perhaps the current increase in accounting wealth (redirection of money supply into financial instruments rather than production and employment) actually results in less money in the average man economy as well as excess money chasing un-earned return on investment. The lesson to be learned from this is that except where individuals are able to create accounting capital (not earned, but fabricated), actual wealth (as measured in physical production return to physical capital) has declined. Since the middle class has little opportunity to participate in the manipulative economy for generating accounting capital, and because that capital is invested less and less in production assets, the security and power of the middle class has necessarily declined.

One reason why many savers are willing to give their money for almost zero interest to banks and government is that prices are not having a negative, and possibly having a positive effect on them. Other savers, unsatisfied or unable to manage with the lack of return have flocked to other riskier investments such as equities and financial instruments which have rebounded since 2007 not because of improved performance and value, but due to desperate investor demand and increased government intervention in the economy. Other less productive means of earning attractive returns in today's economy are insider trading, commission sales (sometimes/often even of foreign products) and government contracting. Since the realistic possibilities for middle class investors to invest in productive small business have been almost eliminated due to the low cost of transportation and labor, universal technical diffusion, economies of scale and regulation/management by government, the main investment alternatives for the middle class now are land, metals and stocks, controlled largely by regulation and manipulation, and not directly related to production.

Reduction of Savings and Inventory

From the earliest days of the history of mankind, savings from prosperous times have been used to ensure survival in times of need. Most people have read the Old Testament story of Joseph in Egypt where he gained great respect from storing grain that was later used to save many from famine. In early colonial days storage and preservation of food and energy sources was essential to prevent starvation and destitution. Even until the mid-20th Century this was a very important practice in rural areas of the United States. In many countries savings were maintained in the form of metals and jewels. Even though people worked within present conditions they recognized that some sort of physical insurance in the form of tradable, usable or edible wealth is required. The result of these practices was that there was always some wealth that could not produce returns. Security for the future was based on savings, not on borrowing, so current conditions controlled the total wealth of society.

After the Depression and World War II when Keynesians and statist utopians had gained broad influence through the use of New Deal programs and international financial networks, the death of natural cycles of all sorts (including economic) and the economic management ability of technicians and brain-trusters (modern day priests) was increasingly proclaimed. In their worldview it was ultimately no longer necessary for individual persons to look after themselves or to waste assets as insurance. The modern day priests would manage the economy so that the economic cycles would decrease (and fffff-fade away - as The Who sang), and when there were unforeseen problems the state would provide relief to the people to ensure their wellbeing.

With confidence in this promise, or rather with the hubris of continued growth and prosperity, validated by the unprecedented economic bonanza that came as a result of the aftermath of World War II, individuals and businesses began to behave in a very un-American and non-traditional way. They began to think that utopia had arrived and there was no need to waste energy worrying about tomorrow or whether desirable any social goals were actually affordable. It was the dawn of the age of the credit card and a society that could ignore its current ability to pay, because it was only borrowing from its rich future self. The new approach to credit was much broader than just borrowing today to pay back tomorrow. In previous stages of financial system development money was borrowed from assets whose earnings could be used to pay off loans, so that all loans were based on a real physical reality. In the case of lay-away purchases the asset itself was held by the seller until the price was fully paid.

Under the new financial structure, credit was issued on the hope or forecast of future income, rather than earnings to assets. This hope was built on the foundation of the new Post-World War II affluence. Since it was not based on an actual reality such as assets, the reality could ultimately be realized or lost. However, with the new faith in the modern day priests to ensure only positive realities, everyone joined in the game. The result of this is that optimistic future income was fully tapped to cover the purchase of goods and services which would not all remain or provide benefits into that same future income flow. This meant that in many cases the situation of many persons would reflect negative wealth if the priests did not deliver on their promises - or if the priests delivered only for the elite and their agents rather than ordinary people.

Since no actual future income exists in the present, it was necessary to modify the system to provide accounting money to cover these transactions. The United States Dollar as the world reserve currency facilitated this by increasing many-fold the Dollars available worldwide. The United States Dollar had to go off the gold standard to allow the unlimited production of Dollars without being limited to the physical gold held to back the paper value. Over decades this system progressed to the stage where the constantly growing money supply itself was used by the priests to remove the need for assets in the calculation of future income in the same way as Henry George assessed the increase in value of land. Now that this structure is fully institutionalized it has begun to control the movements and activities for consumer lifetimes, but are considered to be combined assets and future earnings - the true realization of being on the treadmill of life!

In the business and finance worlds the same concepts brought about similar revolutionary changes. Business could reorient its thinking to goods and services that might not have value in the future since future value is not needed to justify a current purchase based on hoped for future income. Future income would in theory cover any loss of value in current purchase except for the fact that borrowing always has a borrower and a lender. Of course, if future income were less than the value of a current purchase in the future there would be a wealth transfer to the lender, but this possibility was not taken very seriously. Instead the assumption of continuously increasing income drove finance to become a major revenue contributor to business income and to be integrated even into pricing strategy. This new market financing regime at first brought some convenience and efficiency by freeing some current capital and creating additional future-based accounting assets, but this depended on optimistic assumptions.

Even internal business operations were affected by the new financial assumptions. Business previously operated with significant investment in, and income from, replacement parts and components. Under the new financial assumptions inventory was seen as an unnecessary overhead and business began to switch to just in time delivery so that less physical space and investment was necessary. Not only did this reduce the fixed costs, but it also shifted the overhead burden further down the line to suppliers. It also freed business from the continuity restrictions because there would be less cost in changing designs due to the absence of inventory.

This shift to a future orientation in the financial and market systems also had a parallel in the social and religious realms. Whereas traditional religion, particularly Christianity, has emphasized theological systems that encourage present day action for future reward, the latter half of the 20th Century saw a readjustment in religious outlook to concentrate more on current life. This can be seen in the ideas of Liberation Theology which seek to bring the Kingdom of Heaven to the here and now. The new thinking is that good actions will bring good rewards in the present day. Further, there is or should be justice in the here and now, rather than in the life hereafter. In reality, most modern people, including Christians, no longer actually believe in life after death, so they support the need to preserve life at all costs and satisfy desires in this life. This is also like the business model of just in time delivery since treasures are not stored up in heaven for later use, but are borrowed against for current consumption.

The Conspiracy of Mammon: How America Fell on the Slippery Slope to World Dominance

In earlier chapters we saw how social and political rights movements emerged beginning in the 1960s with existential challenges to all traditional middle class values, yet which met no meaningful opposition. At the same time there was a breakdown in physical community and cultural/institutional/professional linkages within the local population; and the emergence of a new present time orientation in financial/philosophical systems. There were also stupid social experiments, fads, absurd academic research, instant gratification consumption of all sorts, excessive regulations, unrealistic standards, pyramids of dependency, attacks on all social structures, psychological disinformation, deceptive marketing, not to mention numerous foolish military adventures and world policing. Promotion of this total change in society became itself a philosophy through the peace/non-violence and anti-establishment movements. Normally, such a total change in a social system to increase access to everything for everyone would not be possible and there would always be winners as well as losers. Yet, for a long time none of this revolutionary change seemed to impose any cost to American prosperity. Since there was no apparent cost there was also no meaningful resistance.

This apparent lack of cost from the revolution was combined with the key social concept of the 1960s, "it doesn't matter," and the new knowledge priesthood was consulted. Economists answered that the colossal waste of time, energy and resources involved in the Post-World War II revolution described in previous chapters had no economic cost since breaking down future consumption and distribution obstacles was actually the very genius of our society that had brought about our prosperity. It was a case of the inmates running the asylum! In fact, almost none of the above-mentioned components of social revolution helped the economy or society, but rather actually destroyed it. Americas Post-World War II prosperity had little to do with production or international trade and yet consumption continued to grow,. Economists explained that American prosperity was actually due to all the fanciful Post-World War II movements and experiments. In fact, this was all an illusion and America's prosperity was only due to the United States Dollar as the world reserve currency. As a result, all the military activities, consumerism and social experiments were not contributing to the base economy and just burning up previously saved assets created under a different social and financial regime. The United States would have been much wealthier if, instead of wasting its false prosperity, it had saved and invested this excess so that when the rainy day comes (like in recent years) it would have had the resources to save itself.

As we have seen, the unique geographical conditions of the United States, time of settlement and power of the middle class are directly responsible for its pre-Depression prosperity. That was the natural prosperity of the United States and was not so dramatically better than that of some other countries (remember the prosperity of parts of Brazil and Argentina in the early 20th Century?). The New Deal policies and programs helped many who had suffered from the Great Depression, but by the time the United States entered World War II the country had not yet fully returned to the prosperity of the 1920s. It was the special conditions that resulted from the Post-World War II period that brought unprecedented and unearned prosperity to the United States - not big government and statist policies.

In fact the Post-World War II experience was totally unnatural. The war economy and Post-World War II boom filled positions in world production that were open only by virtue of the decimation of the European advanced population, by many who would not otherwise had the opportunity or even been qualified. It was that reason and not the so-called American Exceptionalism that was responsible for the tremendous expansion in factory labor with high union wages. Therefore, the problems presented in the preceding chapters were indirectly a result of the destruction of Europe in World War II and the resulting world financial restructuring. As a result, liberals and misfits pushed forward their destructive agenda with no apparent harm to the country, so the natural opposition was not activated. This situation was possible only because of the behind the scene schemes of the power elite and the false prosperity that masked the effects of the liberal agenda.

This situation was an illusion that is now fading as the combined impact of all the wrong-headed, evil and damaging policies of the Post-World War II period come home to roost. The very unnatural prosperity and unreal conditions that allowed the total destruction of traditional American middle class society are seen by many as a result of American Exceptionalism, rather than as the result and tool of power elite plans. Even traditional middle class value holders and conservatives are beginning to able to see the true nature of the false American prosperity and the American Empire.

Therefore, it is deceptive and misleading to consider that the public policies that emerged largely during and after the apogee of American prosperity actually contributed to it. In fact, they reduced it. So the myths of America that prevail today and which now include all the changes that have taken place since World War II are a great hoax created by modern mythmakers. In reality, some of the original, but almost none of the current American myths contributed to and supported American prosperity. Some of the American myths are not only false, but harmful to the nation. The myths of America today are not the myths of America that describe what made America great, but what previously great America has become in its great decline.

Chapter 18. Does Ideology Make a Difference?

Overview

In earlier chapters we have seen the continuous line of unique historical conditions and developments in the United States that have made the American experience unique in world history; and made possible unprecedented freedom and prosperity for most people, especially the middle class. The United States built on the devolution of power to the middle classes in England, and extended this to the majority of the American people. This may explain to some extent the "special relationship" between the United States and the British Peoples, but the prosperity of the two nations are different in nature and are supported by different conditions.

If we consider the British People as living primarily in South Africa, Australia, New Zealand, Canada, Greater Ireland, Great Britain and the United States we can see that to a large extent that except for Great Britain and Greater Ireland, the other countries based their prosperity on similar opportunities flowing from European settlement of sparsely inhabited land largely isolated from European conflicts. Of these only the United States had almost unlimited areas of fertile and temperate land along with other adequate resources. Great Britain and Greater Ireland, prospered from the management of a worldwide colonial empire combined with their technical innovation and industrial base.

Unique land and resource conditions remained powerful in the United States into the late 20th Century, although there were early signs of their limits during the Great Depression and the Dust Bowl experience, and from poor coal/forest resource management. However, the size of the United States and the availability of resources initially, and until after World War II the scope for international trade, largely allowed the ambitious and greedy to pursue wealth and power without directly confronting the middle class. Most military adventures of the United States were almost certainly wars in support of elite rather than national interests, but except for the War of Northern Aggression these were not in or near the homeland, and did not directly harm the domestic economy.

Increased immigration from all countries regardless of their compatibility with historical American culture has now greatly reduced the advantage of physical distance from countries in conflict with the United States since their people are living inside the United States. As a result there are now anti-American demonstration by non-Americans or naturalized Americans within the United States, easy travel to the United States for people who oppose United States policies and the wealth of native-born Americans, and terrorist sleeper cells within the country, so that challenging and unmanageable practical domestic security conditions are becoming similar to those experienced in Europe and other countries for the first time in American history.

After World War II, international policing in peacetime, greatly expanded to serve the now continuously-growing ambitions of the business and finance elite, began to directly affect the middle class through draft conscription during conditions of prosperity. This created a middle class backlash during the Vietnam War years, so that ultimately the middle class was removed from the drafted soldiery. World War II and the Post-War years had firmly set the United States on a path toward an urban society - one that was very much different from its traditional orientation. It is interesting to observe that it was this same period that generated the greatest interest in traditional American culture and society, especially in music and crafts. However, this was short-lived and ultimately the interest could not recreate the physical communities that were no longer home to the majority of the American People and which could define and unite the great American middle class.

We have seen that the suburbanization of America was an additional nail in the coffin of localized institutions. In the place of those local institutions for the first time, a national, rather than local or regional identity emerged which sought to mythologize all the positive and romantic images of American history for the population generally. This was possible because of the unprecedented affluence the nation enjoyed and by the new national urban demography. Yet, almost at the same time when a national identity was formed attacks on all aspects of its historical national myths and identities began and succeeded in a very short period of time. In response to the success of these attacks an effort was made to reconcile the traditional American myths with the radically changed society and political-economic conditions. As a result, popular ideas about American institutions and society may be correct, but popular understanding of their causes, meaning and their association with myths and ideology are now substantially distorted. The nation now uses those myths and ideology for public discourse, decision making and action rather than the direct experience of links between cause and effect.

As we have seen in the previous chapters, America's Post-War prosperity was not due primarily to exceptional hard work, virtuousness or intelligence, although most people believe this to be the case. Americans continue to imagine themselves as hard working, virtuous and intelligent. This self-image may not be true, or at least not be true in comparison with other people. Instead, Americans became complacent, first through prosperity and then through misleading new national myths. That caused them to think that non-Americans, and even some less successful Americans, were less capable and deserving, and that they needed foreign aid, transfer of technology, access to education, opportunity to immigrate to the United States, and affirmative action to help them compete with native-born Americans. All this was due to the myth that non-Americans were not equal to middle class Americans and could never compete with them. In principle Americans would give charity supplements out of their excess that would never result in competition with the recipients or measurable loss to themselves.

Unfortunately, competition and loss has been the exact result of our national policy to extend the American system and benefits to the entire world. Group by group and country by country are adopting the progressive qualities that Americans believed to be unique to themselves, combined with other qualities (such as unethical practices and joint family business) which Americans do not have and which promote success against native-born middle class Americans. Middle class Americans lose on both sides of the coin; we not only do not have many of the myth-based qualities that we aspire to have and also do not have many qualities that actually produce success, especially for success in open global competition. The earlier total faith in national myths has paradoxically led to the proliferation of all manner of non-traditional behavior and mixing of population groups that do not share some of the American myths (including the belief that virtue means allowing the non-virtuous to broadcast their expression with equal consideration), with the result that those myths are self-defeating. This type of paradox results from the practice of many seemingly apparent American virtues - such as democracy, self- expression, the welfare state, etc. - which actually promote challenges to the underlying social contract that made them possible in the first place.

National Delusion

It is difficult to question the myths of America since they are assumed in most social and political discourse. In the period up to the end of the 20th Century it was easy to accept myths because they seemed realistic in light of the simpler conditions that prevailed in the United States. At that time there was a more direct and case by case debate over concrete issues and actions, and myths played a negligible role in policy decisions. However, this situation has changed almost completely in the last several decades. Other countries, such Pakistan and Bangladesh, never seem to truly understand why they have come to be. In the United States such self-questioning was almost non-existent because of the near total acceptance of the basic national myths that did not apparently conflict with accepted practices and values. However, the development of new myths gradually and cleverly linked with the old ones no longer seek to support traditional practices and values, but now openly dispute them, breaking their truthful linkage with national identity.

I would like to challenge the American myths and instead search for direct relationships between facts (actions, policies and conditions) and outcomes. In order to do this I have to state my basic premise that reality, or the framework for social organization, is largely relative and that human society can, under various circumstances, work almost equally successfully under many assumed – even though sometimes contradictory – truths or social realities (myths). At first consideration that may seem to be counter-intuitive since myths should normally be used to *explain* outcomes. In reality, however, myths are often believed to actually *produce* outcomes. Nevertheless, national myths do not of themselves directly produce outcomes, but only are used to explain how a society would like to see itself in those outcomes; what it would aspire to be. That means that almost any myth can be applied to any outcome, although some are more related and appropriate than others. Although myth-making is a very important aspect of national identity, I am not aware of any examples where the essential validity of national myths has been explored in the assessment of American society.

To begin with, the United States is not necessarily prosperous because it has a so-called democratic system of government, although the national myth asserts that the democratic system is the source of its prosperity. In fact, it is possible that if the extent of democracy were reduced the prosperity might be even greater (with more effective management of the natural conditions, history and people of the country). The American myth also asserts that the American population is somehow self-selecting with the present optimal mix of diversity for producing prosperity (even though there has actually been a full range of diversity level over time from nearly none to the present maximum), although different population sizes, distribution and mix might actually be (and have been) more beneficial to the nation. American myth-makers constantly seek to promote extension of various policies and characteristics linked with core myths such as democracy, diversity and free enterprise with the justification that they benefit the society, which in current thought means that they create economic well-being. Yet, I would suggest that there are few direct linkages between those American myths and the actual national well-being.

America is rich (measured in some way with some definition, although this definition, too, may only be a myth) and has a certain political (and possibly an inseparable economic and bureaucratic) system which we consider to be the result of national myths and ideology. Canada (or better yet, India) has another ideology and is poorer, so we consider that its different ideology makes it poorer. In this case our ideology is "us" and their ideology is "them" so "we" are better than "they" are. This means that not just our specific conditions are better but that we ourselves are. So whatever defines us or how we define ourselves becomes our ideology and the basis for explaining our social system and its outcomes. This assumes that if we as a people physically switched places with a people in another country we would more or less replicate our current prosperity, even though we know this is not valid.

Reliance on ideology to make decisions, especially policy decisions, assumes the truth and relationship of a system of ideas, which can (and often does) ignore the importance of actual conditions and structures. If the structures and conditions in different societies are similar the outcomes are also likely to be similar, regardless of their stated ideologies. It is the structures and conditions that determine the outcomes. There are some examples of this such as in the countries of South Asia where there are similar structures and conditions, and differing ideologies, but where the results are not so different. In most countries, such as the United States, though, we often confuse an ideology with independent social, economic and resource structures and conditions, and attribute results and outcomes falsely to that ideology.

The Rise and Fall of Great Powers by Paul Kennedy considers the nature and scale of government and regulation as important factors in the successful functioning of nations. In the United States there was some deviation from the patterns found in that study due to its unique space, resources, individual freedom and middle class power. However, for the United States, in addition to its historically unique situation, the key factors that have determined national wealth creation are currency value; and control of labor and its costs. Historically low cost labor outweighs almost everything else when it can be put to use. Modern government has introduced the added factor of currency value which influences the cost of labor as well as having an independent trade effect. In the United States the democratization of wealth and political power reached its peak and began to decline during the 20th Century as the cost of labor increased.

While the United States largely lost control of its labor pricing after World War II, the day of reckoning was postponed by the Breton Woods agreement which established the United States Dollar as the world reserve currency, and later by the financial system established to recycle Petro Dollars after the Arab Oil Embargo. As a result, labor in most countries was priced cheaply against the dollar and made it possible for even working class Americans to benefit as if they were part of the international management class - which they were indirectly for a time. As long as technology and information were controlled and allocated so as to retain the finishing, organized technical factory production, science, and local services activities for products in the American economy there was a relatively equitable income distribution throughout American society since the economic surplus was used to buy lower cost superfluous imports. The ultimate support for this came from lower values in the currencies of other countries, and the resulting orders of magnitude-less prosperity for the masses in those countries.

Francis Fukuyama's book The End of History was the result of great American and neo-con hubris and built on the flawed assumption of American myths that Americans would always be on top because of their unique characteristics. The book postulated an end to the historical struggle in political economy through American Exceptionalism and universal human market democracy aspirations. However, what we really see at the beginning of the 21th Century is that not only is the myth of American Exceptionalism false, but also that the unlimited group rights claims justified under an American prosperity of a particular time and conditions are irreconcilable and unsustainable. Marxists used to claim that the West was plagued by internal contradictions. Maybe they were more correct than they knew.

Chapter 19. Conclusion

The Judgment of Solomon

I have tried to limit the scope of this book to the unique situation of political economy in the United States in a historical context. It is true that in some ways the United States is representative of European societies, but their specific situations have not been considered in this work. Specific foreign policy and international relations issues have also not been addressed. Broad movements and development in domestic social structure have been identified, but detailed policy and issues have not. In recent years there has been an increase in so-called "single interest" politics and the de-linking of numerous individual issues from consistent mutually-reinforcing "value" packages. In this book I have sought to avoid this distraction.

Since the focus of this book is the political economy of the United States, the most important single subject is the middle class social contract. The key observations made in previous chapters relevant to the social contract are:

1. The wealth of the United States is due less to the productive labor of its people than to its earlier abundant resources and freedom for individual endeavor.
2. The social contract in the United States was due to core European middle class political and family values.
3. The most obvious and routine features of the United States political economy were generally consistent with these values, but faced periodic encroachment on liberty and setbacks from attacks by power elites.
4. The fundamental conflict in American political economy has been the desire of the middle class to maintain its freedom and liberty in daily life against the greedy and power hungry elites at the centers of financial and government power.

5. Most encroachment on the freedom and liberty of the middle class could be repulsed until the latter 20th Century as a result of the presence of an expanding frontier and extensive resources.

6. The end of the frontier and unlimited resources brought a shift in the location of the battlefield of political economy to urban areas and modern industry that are more easily controlled by the power elites.

7. The increased size of government and regulation in the more concentrated modern urban environment reduced the liberty and freedom needed for innovation and resisting power elites.

8. The rapid loss of low-cost labor advantages in the 20th Century presented a major crisis for the United States economy. This crisis was unexpectedly managed for many years as a result of the damage to the world industrial plant during World War II and the Post-War establishment of the United States world financial dominance.

9. American urbanization resulted in class struggles which were ultimately controlled by Post-World War II suburbanization.

10. Urbanization, suburbanization, extension of government scale and regulation, and the emergence of a statist technical-managerial class brought an end to local community-based solidarity and political power.

11. The various group rights movements and their claims on the national political economy, which could only be afforded by the unique and unsustainable advantages of the Post-World War II financial dominance of the United States, and were not significantly opposed due to the lack of any immediate economic hardship, could only produce cumulative irreconcilable damage to the social contract and middle class power after about 40 years.

12. As a result of the breakdown in the social contract, policy debates are now not on issues, but on the identity of the American people and the nature of the republic.

13. Increased immigration after 1965 achieved its hidden purpose of reducing labor costs, destroying national identity and eliminating middle class consensus power to resist the power elites.

14. Concern over the scale of world population and urbanization has almost vanished as power elites have discovered that increased population provides more and cheaper labor, more consumer demand, more constituents to manipulate, more labor for the army and security services, and a check on any middle class or group unity that could stand in the way of elite control.

15. The natural standard of living of the American People was reached prior to the Great Depression and can be expected to return toward that level in the future as the United States Dollar's world reserve currency benefits disappear, and with adjustments due to the greatly increased population, urban society, changes in technology, and government scale and regulation.

16. With the decline of native-born American productivity and cost advantages, the United States economy has been maintained by reduction in labor cost due to increased immigration, low-cost imports and by foreign investment.

17. Globalization is not natural or inevitable, but has been organized and promoted by power elites and their technical-managerial agents in order to gain control over labor and markets at world and local levels. Almost no influence remains over this process outside of the power elite's driving forces. All other groups, including the middle class, must scramble to find any available slots in the global economic structure.

18. Investment by American business has shifted overseas and is the motivating factor behind most current foreign policy.

19. Middle class political power (to achieve either so-called liberal or conservative objectives) is inconsistent with group rights, modern immigration/labor policy, technocratic management, large scale government, modern urbanization, globalization, and multi-national corporations.

20. The technical-managerial class is not itself part of the power elite, but has given up its association with the middle class in order to benefit from the changed political economy. Since this class generally has so-called liberal political views, it appears that the new political economy has a liberal structural objective. In fact, the goal is power and in recent

times the so-called liberal agenda has helped to destroy the power of the middle class which was in the way of this goal. Once achieved, power may be used for liberal or conservative objectives - but by the power elite and not by the middle class.

21. Nearly all current trends in American political economy support the new political economy controlled by the power elite assisted by the technical-managerial class.

22. The quality of life that Americans enjoyed for over 200 years was due principally to the location, space and resources of the United States, the inherited middle class social and economic structure from Great Britain, and most importantly the *lack* of global competition.

23. Domestic competition may have been good for American prosperity and well-being, but global competition has not been. Global hegemony, on the other hand, has been very good for American prosperity.

24. Contrary to American myths, Americans are not fit for equal global or even domestic immigrant competition in the modern economy.

25. New American myths have been developed over the past 50 years when unusual historical conditions prevailed. These encouraged Americans to believe that they were entitled to a high level of prosperity and privilege, never before known in history. This was due to the *lack* of global competition and *despite* recent changes in the American political economy. These myths are false and global competition is resulting in reduced prosperity and well-being for Americans.

26. Prosperity is the foundation of freedom and liberty. In this light freedom and liberty can be considered as assets, ultimately with actual money values. It is difficult to be a debtor and preserve assets. It is difficult to be hungry or unemployed and assert moral and ethical values. It is difficult to retain ownership of assets without money to develop and use them. It is impossible to sell one's labor at the cost of living when that of all others is cheaper. When there is no capital or labor to sell in the market, freedom and liberty are sold - after that the future is only slavery and rebellion.

The Political Economy of the United States Today

The cumulative developments presented in previous chapters and the conditions given above have put into place changes in American political economy which are now starting to have fundamental effects on society as they feed on themselves. The main areas where these effects are felt are: politics, livelihoods, freedom, competence, costs and identity.

Now we are entering a transition period in the United States where the old foundations of independence, cohesion and shared identity that were barely held in place for a time by extraordinary consumerism have collapsed. This is already resulting in major restructuring of the United States economy, polity and even geography (reference the book, The Big Sort by Bishop and Cushing). In the face of this rapid and dramatic restructuring, pundits of different ideological bents claim that this restructuring is alright because the United States is an ideological nation and as such Americans are an exceptional people. We have seen that Americans are not an exceptional people of their own making and that there is no consistent or accurate American ideology. The United States, to the contrary of the claims of pundits, can never be an true ideological nation, but must function primarily at the level of defensive livelihoods, community, family, social relations and daily living. It can only be an ideological nation to the extent that ideology supports those defensive livelihoods.

I have tried not to focus on the detailed examples of specific individuals, groups or organizations in order to provide a broad view of development in the United States during nearly 300 years. I also wanted to avoid distracting the reader with ambiguous and over-used terms and concepts that would divert his thought to preconceived judgments. However, here I must mention one specific subject which has been widely distorted and continuously dismissed, but which otherwise often provides valuable and important information worthy of careful consideration: conspiracy theory.

Whenever someone tries to link different activities with a common negative outcome they are almost inevitably tarred with the name of conspiracy theorist; whereas if the outcome were good they might be called consensus-builders. This is strangely inconsistent and is the result of another myth; namely that people are naturally good and generally work together for good outcomes. I would argue that people naturally seek to achieve benefits for themselves and only work with others when they need to. In the United States, middle class consensus made personal and community benefits congruent for the dominant population, so cooperative civic behavior for the common good was the norm. As a result of the early suppression of power elites in America the empowered middle class saw the occasional power elite grab for its rights and prosperity as a deviation from the normal behavior prevailing since the American Revolution.

However, as the American social contract has collapsed self-interest has become less related to common benefit, so it is not surprising that interest groups form to promote their objectives which by their definition are not for the common good. Since modern communications allow much improved information management and coordination independent of communities, it should not be surprising that capable groups are arising to promote almost every self-interest known to man. Although terms like collusion and insider trading still have negative connotations, they certainly do not receive the same immediate and scornful reception as does conspiracy theory. Somehow the idea of system-level and ambitious economic, social or political plans that are not shared by visible public groups is considered to be either foolish or beyond the capacity of outsiders to perceive.

For the purpose of this book I use the concept of power elites and their objectives rather than the negatively perceived term conspiracy theory. Since power elites by definition have power in the form of money and influence, it is inconceivable that they cannot hire the best brains, bribe the most powerful and implement the broadest plans to gain increased wealth and control. The loss of the voting majority middle class, collapse of the social contract and the lack of belief that the power elite engages in hostile organized efforts against the common good means that there is no longer any significant opposition to efforts by the power elite to structure all institutions of the political economy for their benefit. The old expressions "get your foot in the door" and "going down a slippery slope" describe this state of affairs.

Whether the power elite directly plan and bring about developments, or whether these developments happen through their indirect influence of independent factors is not so important as the fact that they are the major beneficiaries. We have seen that in the past conditions were suitable to satisfy the greed of the power elite even while allowing the broad middle class to enjoy unprecedented prosperity, but that now the greed of the power elite and changed conditions make it useful and possible for the power elite to destroy the middle class and expropriate its wealth and power for itself. It is not necessary that the power elites be the only beneficiaries, since they need foot soldiers in this work who must also be rewarded. So any group useful to destroy the middle class consensus can be at least temporarily useful .

With this situation in mind we can now observe and assess the practical manifestation of the disempowerment of the middle class in several aspects of the current political economy.

1. Politics
The collapse of the social contract and power of the middle class means that the near universal electorate is now split into numerous

vote blocs, most of which are antagonistic to each other and - far from being like the ever expanding pie of Adam Smith - which have the goal to actually extract privilege and financial power from other groups. At the same time the power elites in government, business and institutions have used this situation to bolster their independent status and power beyond the control of any single voting bloc. Now the political system has degenerated into winning the majority from individual vote blocs rather than from individual voters.

This is particularly notable in the case of Barack Obama who was able to collect a new group of vote blocs including foreign-born and mixed race voters. No matter which party or candidate wins an election there is now no majority in place to force the implementation of its desired policies. To the extent that they do not answer to any voting majority, elected officials can defy many vote blocs and even a plurality of voters on almost any issue. Power elites who can provide campaign funding, future employment and other inducements are able to directly influence elected officials to accommodate their wishes with no direct opposition recourse for the majority of voters. This situation has resulted in the disgraceful and un-American manifestation of the alien parliamentary system practice of the rich and famous relocating or dislocating to jurisdictions for the sole purpose of being elected, such as with Rockefeller, Kennedy, Clinton, Bush as other lesser lights.

Government agencies are now probably more important than elected officials in practical application of state control because they develop and implement rules. Rules are much more numerous and probably more important than laws, and are almost completely outside of the range of influence of general voters. Although government institutions have various public consultation procedures, these are limited to certain actions and policies, and no serious response is required even in the face of significant opposition. Since elected officials are not accountable to the voters except at elections and rules are made by unaccountable and professionally insulated government staff on a daily basis, it is not possible for the general public to influence the form or enforcement of rules. Of even more concern is the use of so-called professional or ethical codes and practices followed by government institutions in the absence of any direct and formal public review and approval.

The result of this situation is that political ideology is not consistent, is packaged for individual vote blocs, is not accountable and is discretionary in application by bureaucrats. Candidates may differ in some of their positions, but most will not deliver a package according to the wishes of the general voting public. Moreover, only special individuals will choose to be candidates as a result of the expense required, and the intense media scrutiny and critique imposed. This means that grass roots candidates in touch with the general public and not beholden to the power elite are unlikely to step forward. It is generally the hard core ambitious, ruthless and shameless who are now attracted to politics.

I have mentioned earlier that global competition is not beneficial to American prosperity. In contrast, domestic competition allowed Americans to "vote with their feet" and provided the general public some leverage over business interests. In the same way, political competition, when it was localized and directly accountable to the voters, provided a method to achieve some satisfaction for the voting majority. However, as the population has grown and institutions have been alienated from community the bureaucratic state has taken over. With the advent of vote blocs political competition now is largely concerned with who in the power elite benefit most.

2. Livelihoods
No matter what other conditions prevail in a society, livelihood is the most important issue in human life. Without the resources to control important aspects of life such as home, food, mobility, children, basic consumption and relations with other community members an

individual becomes a slave. The key elements of livelihood are: choice in type, time, location and duration of work. As we have seen in earlier chapters, Americans have historically had unprecedented choice in these.

Since there was an overall shortage of labor throughout most of American history, largely due to the possibility of own-account labor and entrepreneurship, there was generally a choice of type of work because most labor could be substituted for different jobs. This meant that a man could work on his own farm, become a tractor mechanic in a small town or work as a factory foreman with the same qualifications. In recent years, however, this is increasingly impossible since more specific certifications are required for each job and doing own-account work is increasingly regulated and requires higher investment. Now it is more difficult to substitute labor and change from one type of work to another.

In the past convenient and complimentary part-time and seasonal work was possible because of farm activities. Since labor was in short supply and the farm schedule also influenced industrial demand, it was possible to organize the economy and even the government (legislature and schools for example) according to the seasons. That allowed some self-reliance on own-account activities as well as participation in the wage economy. Today this system has largely vanished. Increased seasonal and part-time work is the result of increased labor/reduced demand, but without balancing own-account activities. This is largely due to urbanization, unprecedented immigration and increased requirements for work credentials.

With the transition to an urban society, expenses such as insurance, utilities and all consumption are continuous and require a life-long seamless revenue stream in the form of wage income. When non-urban and own-account activities were more common, they could provide supplemental consumption, income and asset growth as seasonal, part-time or even for varying durations as stop-outs from the wage economy. The presence of continuous expenses makes other than full-time work an option only for the privileged or those under duress.

The books, The Big Sort, Coming Apart, and also Paradise Road by David Brooks explain how people in the past several decades have moved to areas throughout the country in such a way that their social and political orientation matches with their neighbors. It is suggested that in the past there was a wide range of social and political opinions in most jurisdictions, but that this range is becoming much more narrow today. Since these social and political opinions are also connected with occupation and income, these characteristics are also becoming geographically isolated. This means that not all jurisdictions provide the same range of work, residence and lifestyle opportunities that they once did. Coupled with the decline in non-urban and own-account activities, this increasingly forces lower skilled "decent native-born folk" and new immigrants into income segregated areas with the hard core poor and anti-social elements. Reduced choices for livelihood and location, and the increased cost of resettlement and job acquisition mean that changing job location is becoming more difficult for the vast majority of families who are without specialized skills - and even with the wrong opinions.

In addition to the above detrimental changes in the livelihood of the American worker, the introduction of the two-income family structure has dramatically increased the labor pool, particularly of the less skilled. Moreover, the more urban and sedentary nature of work, coupled with changes in the family structure makes women more attractive for employers - and men less so. This reduces the job market for men and the less skilled, except in more constrained environments where physical labor or just warm bodies are required.

The control of the labor market by the power elite has been made complete by the unprecedented volume of immigration, particularly from groups whose family structure allows pooling of incomes and expenses; and community networking/support unlike the traditional way of life for native-born Americans. Examples of this are immigrant families where 5-10 members all have some income and live under the same roof sharing the same expenses; and parents of immigrants who work in wage jobs even though they have been sponsored as dependents. All of these factors make livelihood increasingly impossible for the general native-born public. The inevitable result of this is resentment, anti-social activity and an increased need for support from the welfare state.

Government activities that effect the general public have expanded greatly, have become fulltime and require continuous compliance. The result of this is a much higher and continuous burden of tax on the general public such that a greater part of earnings as well as national wealth must devoted be to government operations for which there is no alternative. This makes it necessary for the public to work more time and to avoid periods with no earning.

3. Competence

Another key component of the American myth is the rugged individualist, the hero who rides off into the sunset, the World War II rivet girl, the inventive farmer and the frontiersman. The "can do attitude" and "necessity is the mother of invention" are staples of the film industry. The idea is that strength of character, commitment, drive and virtue can produce winning results against mere power and even technology (although even technology should respond to American virtue and sincerity). That myth has been converted over time to that of the effective expert. Probably this started with the FDR New Deal technocrats and progressed into the Kennedy Brain Trusters.

Since no one stopped it, this American myth was converted more broadly into the requirement for qualifications such as professional registrations, certificates, etc. This process continued in education, as noted by Wallenstein, where degrees in pseudo-scientific disciplines became increasingly important. From the 1980s onward there was an increasing near-worship of business leaders, financiers, economists and other professionals as their activities became more unfamiliar to the general public. The vocabulary of government officials, particularly in economic, foreign relations, military and security agencies became so distorted that the whole class appeared to be like priests who alone were able to understand and use knowledge to organize the national political economy.

Finally, the computer and Internet revolutions introduced entire systems whose control and even use were not even visible to the general public. This allowed the scorned and socially inept "geeks" and "nerds" to gain respectability, power and even great wealth. Awe of the expert now even extends to all manner of social misfits and immigrants associated with the information industry. It is believed that certain technical education and specializations are the keys to this mysterious art and that the practitioners are somehow nice and well-meaning people.

The above mentioned groups have become America's new priesthood by virtue of having professions that the common man cannot understand. In earlier chapters we have seen that the power elite and their techno-managerial agents are separated from the embattled middle class, the working class and the entitlement class.

The group rights movements have ensured that nearly all groups in society now have more equal representation by except in the military, security and prison populations. This means that instead of selection by ability, selection is done by group association. Of course over the past fifty years this policy, with its cumulative effect from interrelationships, has resulted in much lower national abilities and performance than if it had been otherwise merit-based. This is a cost to the society that is hard to measure except to some extent in the poor service, judgment and quality of results that are achieved, particularly in the government and corporate sectors.

For the middle and working classes, the damage from group rights and from lack of job security has meant that less can be invested in any job, and frequent change of job and organization restructuring means that much experience-based capacity and institutional memory is lost - due to just in time ability. Gradually the situation facing both the middle class and the working class is becoming the same, as ordinary jobs for ordinary people are reduced and lowered in status. International competition and competition from immigrants can only mean that there is little hope for job quality and secure livelihoods for these classes whose members are becoming like gypsies in search of new opportunities.

The new economy is creating changes and stresses in the class structure in the United States. An insecure middle/working plurality class that supports an entitlement class; a knowledge class that has no broader social affiliation or accountability; and a power elite using techno-managerial agents to control the rest. There are few common social/cultural role models to avoid being a ward of the state or in total servitude except those of gaining power, implementing power, or being exempt from control. In this new structure there is little room for civic contributions, shared values, decent families and high standards for the general public. There is no rugged individualist common man in today's society.

4. Identity

The loss of cultural, ethnic, and religious group affiliation for most Americans has been a gradual process sometimes even over more than two centuries. The role of traditional group affiliations was replaced with "civil religion" somewhat akin to French Nationalism. The civil religion was really the transfer of core common values and behavior guidance away from religion - not in opposition to religion - to civic and government institutions. This hardly reduced the power of community values, but instead allowed these to be enforced by the community, rather than the church, informally, and through the formal offices of government. Where informal enforcement was possible, government gave way or even supported the community. When formal enforcement was required government reinforced community values.

It is hard to identify the cause of the recent breakdown in these common community values. It is in part due to the end of physical communities in the urban and suburban environments. It is also due to the independent status given to the steadily more sophisticated market communications and propaganda which claimed to be value-free, but ultimately challenged most community values. Of course, the splintering of the national population into numerous natural and interest groups is the most harmful. The groups rights movements started out as movements opposed to active harmful discrimination within the structure of civil religion described above. However, response to these movements has now advanced to the stage where no discrimination at all is possible from the direction of any common traditional values, but where any minority group values can receive positive discrimination. Not only can government not promote common traditional values, but it is even difficult for the community itself to promote common values publicly or even in private thought.

Following a strategy given in Saul Alinsky's Rules for Radicals and by Mao Tse Tung, the style of public debate has evolved to one where the argued point and its immediate objective is always changing with no logical sequence in order to confuse the opponent and to keep him off balance. As an example, when a majority supports a traditional value it may be condemned as old fashioned or discriminatory, or oppressive to a minority, but when any number support a non-traditional value, activists support enforcement of that value against traditional values, claiming that it is necessary because the new value is "right".

Since there are no longer common physical and value communities, and the modern world encourages isolated, anomic lifestyles, with market supply of buffet styles and behaviors, it is hardly surprising that there are also no longer common role models and aspirations, other than to be rich and famous. This has been explored in a number of sociological studies such as <u>Bowling Alone</u> and several books on the decline of baseball as the American national pastime. This creates the environment where there are no natural leaders and which can produce and encourage demagogues and tyrants.

The crisis of leadership is an international phenomenon and is also related to the inability of political structures to respond to unprecedented population sizes, public services, and scope of information. Despite the much larger management scale, the United States still has only one Congress, one President for almost 320 million people compared to the same structure for 4 million people when the Constitution was enacted. Obviously the performance demands and power are much greater now.

5. Freedom
The splintering of the United States population into group rights vote blocs without common social values, centralizing non-transparent activities in the hands of an unaccountable techno-managerial class, and increased organizational level of society and scale of government mean that ordinary individuals can no longer determine their destiny. When this is coupled with the change from local to global markets, large scale economic operations, and the financial manipulation of asset and labor valuation, there are only three conditions possible for an individual: to set the rules and values, to accept the rules and values, or to somehow be exempt from the rules and values.

As a result of group rights and a statist political structure a majority of the United States population cannot exist peacefully without subsidies, special privileges or payoffs. The meaning of this is that not all current residents of the United States are reconciled in a social contract, but that claim and conflict have been managed by indirect state compensation through taxes or other common costs.

With the decline of the American economy and society there are now inadequate resources to maintain and expand this compensation. That shifts the funding of compensation to direct exaction from vulnerable targets. When some get new rights and privileges others will directly lose them and pay for the loss. Freedom and rights are neither an ever-expanded pie nor a win-win situation. With no social contract the state must adjudicate according to its caprice. Accordingly, the selfishness and disunity of the American political economy provides the state structure for curtailing freedom to any group for use at any time. It may be that freedom will continue to be curtailed gradually, or it may take place quickly since the power of the middle class to resist has been destroyed. The question now is which groups will win and which will lose - and can any new alliance be formed to resist?

For those who must accept the rules and values with no possibility to object or resist, rights have been continuously eroded as the power elite exerts its manipulation and control over more and more aspects of the formal economy so that the only remaining independent assets of the common man are public assets and freedom. Yet those assets are also coveted by the power elite. Already, many formerly public assets such as public space, freedom of speech, public services and natural resources have been transferred into the private sector domain of cost pricing and commercialization. When this happens the general public loses because the very nature of public assets is that they present a common price to all in order to produce the most value from universal use. Increasingly unit pricing for public assets is being introduced so that private bidders may offer a higher price (or exert influence) for individual parts of public assets than that paid by the general public. This concept is an extension of the theory of economic efficiency which is now also being applied in practice to the political realm through group rights movements.

In the same way, when the United States as a debtor nation no longer has the income to cover its debts, it will have to allow the use, control and ownership of its assets, including freedom, by its creditors. Many will counter this assertion with the response that creditors remain willing to loan money to the United States with no collateral, and that in any event freedom could never be exchanged for financial debt. Of course this represents ignorance and naiveté since even recent events show how national and individual freedom can be compromised when debts cannot be paid. A preview of coming attractions message to the United States public should be clear to all when American protestors wanted to exercise their freedom of expression about the International Monetary Fund, Wall Street and the Government of Red China, and were prevented by their own government. This was at a time when no visible debt repayment crisis was evident and is only the tip of the iceberg revealing the sale and loss of freedom to come when debts visibly cannot be repaid.

Sen. Lindsey Graham has suggested that freedom of expression should be curtailed if it endangers United States troops overseas. Since United States troops are stationed almost everywhere in the world and everyone is offended by something, ultimately this would end freedom of speech for all except the power elites. Such a suggestion by a sitting United States Senator is a fearless testing of the waters by the power elites for their intention to confiscate freedoms from the common man as they break free from earlier moderating traditions of middle class power.

Maybe America as represented by the United States never previously existed as a nation, but only as an occasional and partial confluence of interests. There was, however, always an identifiable middle class which gave its ethos to the nation. If the United States is viewed structurally as the pinnacle of Western and world middle class historical development rather than as a nation, its current situation and future should be viewed very differently than it is in common wisdom. If the United States is not a real nation, but only a common market of different groups, if the structure and affluence needed to maintain that common market are no longer present, and if the common middle class ethos no longer exists, what is the way forward?

In recent years some developed the fantasy that the Tea Party Movement might somehow turn the tide of events and restore America to its earlier status. The basis for this was the newly coined concept of so-called American Exceptionalism. Extreme free-market business ideological infiltration of conservative and tea party movements in recent years has resulted in a distortion of history into new myths such as American Exceptionalism. Unfortunately, American Exceptionalism does not address the fundamental problem of the loss of a middle class majority with substantial shared behavior, ideology, regional identity and willingness to make ultimate sacrifices (wealth, ridicule, jail and death), necessary to radically reshape the country.

After about the Year 2000 most culture/knowledge elites on both left and right have made some kind of Faustian bargain with the power elites, except for Congressman Ron Paul, a few unexpected anti-heroes like Noam Chomsky and some people behind the Occupy Wall Street (OWS) movement. Indeed it is the more extreme libertarian and left that may best see the threat from the power elite and be willing to take action to resist it. The groups that see that control by the power elites is no longer tolerable do not understand that even their existence as fringe groups is a result of the broader effort by power elites to control society, population and the economy by fragmenting them. Moreover, the extreme left maintains a disdain for the middle class and could never re-establish a social contract in America. Libertarians also lack an association with the traditional middle class.

Are we actually witnessing the end of the traditional American political economy as some have speculated? If that means that certain unique historical traditions and values no longer hold sway in society, the end has been in progress for a considerable time. If that means that the historical middle class is no longer the dominant force and ethos in America the answer is an unequivocal yes. Why then do things somehow seem to still seem familiar and manageable?

The answer is that human history rarely shows complete overnight changes and as a result it is difficult to ascertain when combined incremental changes result in a fundamental or complete change. This is because institutions and knowledge have substantial continuity in any given society. It is within rather than against the status quo that changes are usually made, but there does come a time when the combined changes within the status quo shift the balance to the point where the fundamental character of the society changes. That change may have already taken place, but has not been perceived yet. The functions of institutions are important, but belief in institutional myths is even more important since it can live longer than actual institutional functions.

Today even many of the biggest critics of the current state of America consider that changing a few laws, a few court justices and some new elected representatives will save the country since the underlying institutions are sound. However, the cumulative effect of changes in the American political economy have resulted in a situation where many or most rights have been converted into privileges that may be suspended. Rights are certain, but privileges are voluntary. Freedom is not a theory, it is a practice. When people think they have freedom they should test it against opposition. If freedom is experienced it may not be a right, but only the lack of any other claimant or opposition. How much freedom can stand up against opposition today? Do you have the freedom to start your own business without hindrance from others or the government? Of course not. Do you have the freedom to voice any political or value opinion on your own or on public property? Of course not? So these are not rights, but privileges.

Since it is clear that the historical United States has been fundamentally changed and is now supported by new myths, administration and value systems, we might ask, is anything of the present America worth preserving and restoring. This is a really good question, especially since Americans have been living an unnatural dream life based on myths describing a reality they have not seen or experienced. Of course we would like to restore our prosperity and life at the head of the world. But since this was an unnatural and undeserved situation, it cannot be restored. Present conditions are a transition back to a previous lower level of affluence, but the social contract and society that fit that earlier time have vanished.

As the late Samuel Huntington suggested in his controversial book, Who Are We?, popular opinion no longer has a clear idea of what constitutes America or the United States as a nation or a "we". The fundamental difficulty is not only to understand *who* we are, but *what* we are - is it a nation, a national economy, a market, a common living group, or just believers in a common myth?

Now we must not only seriously consider who we really are, but who we need to be in the emerging era of a return to a lower level of more realistic and historical affluence. Our traditional myths were based on a different society and a different people and current myths are based on the fleeting American Empire reality of empty consumerism and multi-culturalism. That, too is changing as the presidential primary and general election results of the past year show. What we need today is a new identity, social contract and political economy that can lead us into a new less hubristic era. This is not possible without a dominant and viable middle class with a common ethos. The meaningful question before the nation today is whether a majority middle class consensus and political power can be recreated or can be created anew - or are we trapped by history?

www.ingramcontent.com/pod-product-compliance
Lightning Source LLC
Chambersburg PA
CBHW050440290526
45786CB00006B/2105